GOD IS ON
THE ROAD

GOD IS ON THE ROAD

You, God and the Highway

Paul Dixon, PhD

WESTBOW
PRESS®
A DIVISION OF THOMAS NELSON
& ZONDERVAN

Unless otherwise stated, all scripture quotations are taken from the New Revised Standard Version Bible: Catholic Edition, copyright © 1989, 1993 the Division of Christian Education of the National Council of the Churches of Christ in the United States of America. Used by permission. All rights reserved.

Scripture taken from the King James Version of the Bible.

WestBow Press books may be ordered through booksellers or by contacting:

WestBow Press
A Division of Thomas Nelson & Zondervan
1663 Liberty Drive
Bloomington, IN 47403
www.westbowpress.com
844-714-3454

ISBN: 978-1-9736-9918-7 (sc)
ISBN: 978-1-9736-9919-4 (hc)
ISBN: 978-1-9736-9920-0 (e)

Library of Congress Control Number: 2023909895

Print information available on the last page.

WestBow Press rev. date: 09/06/2023

For Frances, Christina, Scott and Sophia.

CONTENTS

THE ROAD AHEAD

This book uses the extended metaphor of driving to focus on the inner pilgrimage, a journey we are all called to make. Both believers and unbelievers travel the highway of life—experiences of driving lead to reflections on living.

We live at a time when, for many, believing in God seems foolish. Vast numbers reject organised religion. In addition, some only believe in God intellectually without believing in him experientially. If there is a God, the unbeliever is unaware of this divine reality. If there is no God, every believer from every religion (past, present and future) is deluded. That would include me, perhaps you, some of your family and friends, and countless others.

You are reading a Christian spiritual book, yet relevant for all searching for love. God is 'no old man in the sky'. Christians believe God is Love. I hope this book functions like a pair of divine driving glasses, helping you glimpse God's presence on the highway of life. It is a simple book. Nevertheless, if the word/concept 'God' is a stumbling block for you, try substituting 'God' with the phrase 'Spirit of Love'. The latter functions more as a verb (a doing) than a noun (a naming). Thinking of God as a verb is not new; it is found within the Christian tradition.

If you choose to read the chapters in the order they are presented, that's fine. Yet, apart from the introduction and conclusion, the order in which you read the chapters and individual reflections is unimportant. Indeed, a helpful approach is to glance through the thematic or subject index and pick a topic that catches your attention.

Consider making a home for this book in your car, dipping into it when you have quiet moments. If you have the ebook version, you can dip into a reflection almost anytime, anywhere. Wherever and whenever you read this book, please *take your time*—read slowly and ponder. Use the book to reflect on life's journey—*your love story*. Your reflections might lead you to God.

1

JOURNEYS

A to B as perfectly as possible
(Virtues)

A driving instructor once explained how he would practise driving from two points—A to B—as perfectly as possible. It is laudable to seek to be the best we can be. The adage 'practice makes perfect' is not necessarily true, but practice does help make something permanent. On the highway of life, like learner drivers, we need *corrected* practice rather than practising our faults. How's your driving? What changes can you make to live better?

Talk of perfection reminds me of the virtues. A virtuous person is an excellent person. A virtue is a good habit, and a vice is a bad habit. The more you do something, the more it becomes ingrained. We can acquire virtues and vices; this is true of driving as it is of life. St John Henry Newman tells us, '[T]o live is to change, and to be perfect is to have changed often.' A driving instructor might manage to drive perfectly for a mile or two, maybe a little more if he is an expert, but as for life, we all have our faults. Our goal, nevertheless, is to 'Be perfect, therefore, as [our] heavenly Father is perfect.' (*Mt* 5:48)[1] We all fall short, yet we have a God who instructs us with infinite love.

What virtues and vices do you recognise in your own life? Come on; you have some! Whatever they are, aim to drive life's daily A to B as perfectly as possible. We have a great instructor! In striving for perfection and humbly accepting our faults, we grow in virtue and holiness by grace.

Direction, sense of
(Happiness)

As a driver, how is your sense of direction? Are you able to find your way when others are lost? Can you sense the general direction, even when the precise route is unclear? More importantly, how good is your sense of direction on the highway of life?

Human beings are created for true happiness, found only in love. The many decisions we make, some big, others seemingly insignificant, can move us towards achieving authentic happiness and fulfilment. As theists, we believe this is only found in a life lived in harmony with God—*God is Love*. Living in a relationship with God requires trust that He is with us as we travel life's highway. We'll get lost from time to time, but God's love always draws us gently towards Himself, giving direction.

It can be tempting to think we are going in the wrong direction when one is alone; life's highway is bumpy and seems endlessly uphill. Having negotiated the Garden of Gethsemane junction (*Mt* 26:36-46), Jesus trusted and responded to the Father's love and journeyed the ultimate road of love to Calvary. We also need to trust that love will be with us one junction at a time on the highway of life. In the words of St John Henry Newman:

Lead, kindly light, amid the encircling gloom,
Lead thou me on;
The night is dark, and I am far from home;
Lead thou me on
Keep thou my feet; I do not ask to see
The distant scene; one step enough for me.

Journeys

Journey beginning (Happiness)

Why do we drive, ride or walk? Why do we do anything? What will we find in tapping into our inspiration for starting a journey? We might be travelling to work, visiting family, going on holiday, or enjoying a solitary walk. A common thread underpins all our journeys, both on the road and along the highway of life. We want to be happy!

Are you happy? Could you be happier deep down in your very being, your essence, your soul? Aquinas taught that when we choose what makes us truly happy, it leads to God, but when we choose what does *not* make us truly happy, it leads away from God.

St Augustine said, 'Thou hast formed us for Thyself, and our hearts are restless till they find rest in Thee [God]'. Is God at the beginning of your journeys through life?

Journey planning (Trust)

You know how it is: you are going on a journey, so you work out a route. You might circle places on a map, marking points to your planned destination. Things, however, rarely go to plan. Roadblocks make you take a diversion, weather conditions slow you down, and other road users may bump into you, perhaps even try to force you off the road. Yet, one's journey would be aimless without some plan. It is the same with life; we need a plan, but a flexible one. Where are your marked circles as you contemplate your journey through life? The roadblocks on life's highway that frustrate *your* plans by taking you on detours *may* be the roads God wants you to travel. Be patient and have faith. In the future, you will be better able to discern the hand of God, the hand of love, at work in your current present.

In his famous 2005 Stanford University graduation speech, the late Steve Jobs spoke about the importance of following one's passion. 'You've got to find what you love. . . . As with all matters of the heart, you'll know when you find it.' Jobs also spoke of the need to trust in the direction you take since it is only having arrived will things make sense. 'You can't connect the dots looking forward; you can only connect them looking backwards. You have to trust the dots will somehow connect in your future.'

What is *your true heart's desire?* What are you *genuinely* passionate about? Is your heartfelt desire/passion helping you circle-dot the map of your future life? Jim Manney, S.J. in *What Do You Really Want*, explains that a critical insight of Ignatius of Loyola was that discovering what we *really* want is to discover what God wants for us since God places these desires in our hearts. This truth applies to everyone, yes, everyone, including you!

As a child, I loved doing numbered dot-to-dot pictures, keen to discover the image that lay hidden. I occasionally struggled to find the next dot and sometimes got them out of sequence. Yet by the end, I could usually make out the image—even if a little distorted through my mistakes. Following the mapped dots of our life's unknown, we journey in trust, knowing we will get some of the dots wrong. Nevertheless, by following our heartfelt passion and pursuing what we *really* want, we will have sketched upon the canvas of life a portrait of our true self, the person God wants us to be.

Journey or pilgrimage (Pilgrimage)

Pilgrimages are popular. As well as the traditional pilgrimages to destinations such as the Holy Land and Mecca, we have celebrities 'going on pilgrimage' and sharing their experiences on television. In addition, everyday walking and driving can become mini pilgrimages when used to pray—whether stilling the mind or focusing it on discerning the workings of God in one's life.

Life itself is, of course, the ultimate pilgrimage. On the pilgrimage of life, journey and destination coalesce. Journeying with God, the pilgrim lives 'thy kingdom come thy will be done on earth as it is in heaven'. God's kingdom of love is both a future perfect reality and a present imperfect reality. 'Run when you can, walk if you have to, crawl if you must but never give up' is a famous inspirational quote. It applies to the spiritual life too. Although never giving up is excellent advice, the spiritual journey will require changes to routes if they are not leading to the God of love.

The gravestone dash (—) between the date of birth and the date of death reminds us of the importance of making the most of life—*your dash!* 'The Dash' poem by Linda Ellis addresses this very point. On a pilgrim's tombstone, the dash functions more like an arrow (→), pointing the way through death's door to one's heavenly destination→the God of love. Whether one thinks dash or arrow, the following gravestone verse reminds us all to live life as best we can:

> *Remember me as you pass by,*
> *As you are now, so once was I,*
> *As I am now, so you must be,*
> *Prepare for death and follow me.*

Journey homeward (Vocation)

Homeward bound! Finding one's vocation in life brings a sense of coming home, belonging, a feeling that you are where you are supposed to be, doing what you are supposed to be doing. Where is the *path of love* leading you? Who are you? What were you born to be? Your adventure of a lifetime is *your vocation in love.* In calling you home, what is the God of Love asking you to begin, continue, and complete?

Kids—'Are we there yet?' *(Death)*

As parents know, car journeys combined with young children are challenging. 'Are we there yet?' soon reverberates from the backseats. We undertake various projects on life's journey, whether in our work, families or broader social interests. All take time and effort to bring to completion. We need patient perseverance to 'get there' and 'get the job done'. We also need encouragement.

The affectionately named 'Nearly There Trees' is on the A30 road near the Devon and Cornwall border (proper name: Cookworthy Knapp). It is a copse of beech trees on a hill, and for many, they signify that one's Cornish destination is not far away. They also offer an answer to, 'Are we there yet?' In life, the metaphoric 'Nearly There Trees' help as we journey towards achieving our goals, especially when the end seems far off. Notice them.

For the elderly and terminally ill, life's 'Nearly There Trees' are on the horizon—*they are a blessing.* Not all of us will have such a marker; for many, the wheels of life suddenly stop without us knowing. *Your* journey's end may come sooner than you expect. When you 'get there', will you be ready?

Hitchhikers
(Judging)

Thumbs up! You don't see much hitchhiking nowadays. Hitchhiking resonates with the truth that we are all pilgrims in life; we stand on our own two feet, yet intrinsic to life's journey is giving and receiving help. Safety concerns, however, can thwart both the asking for a lift and the goodwill to provide it.

As a child, I remember my parents giving a particular hitchhiker a lift. He was in the Royal Air Force (RAF). He wore his uniform when hitchhiking back to barracks because, he said, it encouraged people to stop—as indeed did my parents. They liked what they saw. His hitchhiking tactic says a lot about how society judges by appearance. Half a century has passed since we gave the smart-looking RAF man a lift. One will never know how the roads of life have treated him since.

Other than for safety reasons, the next time you drive past a hitchhiker, ask yourself why you didn't stop. Offer a prayer or a kind thought for the stranded pilgrim. If he is wearing a tattered old RAF coat, I think I know who it might be.

Trams
(Free will)

Following their tracks, trams have to follow the swept path. Other road users choose which way to go. Christians believe humanity has free will; most people think this too. Moral responsibility requires free will. Nevertheless, how much cause and influence is there on our actions? Consider four areas: genetics, environment, social conditioning, and psychology. Can you see some of your character traits in your parents and perhaps your children? Are you happier when the sun shines and grumpier in the mornings?

Why do people follow different religions while some have no faith at all? How much do anticipated consequences affect your choices? Whatever influences us from without and within, we choose our response. We are not passive victims of fate. The famous theoretical physicist and cosmologist Stephen Hawking noted that people who believe in predestination and that we cannot change things still watch for traffic before crossing the road. Why are you reading this book?

Bollards
(Saints)

Automatic bollards rise from and lower into the ground. They only permit entry for vehicles fitted with an electronic detection pass. Automatic bollards keep unauthorised vehicles out. Do not try a follow-on by driving close behind an authorised car. Whether or not the gates of heaven have automatic bollards, you will not gain entry disguised as someone else. Why even try? You already have a pass; just be yourself. God will recognise you, and the bollards will lower. Saintliness is being the person God is calling you to be.

Roads

National network (Decisions)

Consisting of motorways and primary roads, the United Kingdom's national network of roads links up major towns; they are of regional and national significance. All other roads are non-primary; they are, in a sense, of less importance. Nevertheless, we need non-primary roads for the completion of our journeys.

Suppose motorways and primary roads represent our big

decisions in life, such as getting married, making a career choice and deciding where to live. In that case, non-primary roads represent our small daily decisions. These small decisions build on and complete our big decisions. For the most part, we live on non-primary roads. Yet, do not underestimate the ordinary—it is of divine significance in building up the kingdom of love. What are the motorways and primary roads in your life? Are they linking well with your non-primary roads?

Old roads, old junctions (Gratitude)

I find myself driving past a particular junction that used to take me to a spiritual friend, who has now passed away. She lived alone for many years with her series of sheepdogs, all named Simon-Peter. The last one was Simon-Peter IV. With age, her eyes were not as good as they once were. She often prepared a spread of teacakes or other titbits when I visited. On one visit, my dear friend was not enjoying her morsel—no surprise, as she was eating Simon's dog biscuit! Give thanks for those who have helped you on life's journey. Enjoy your memories and let them enrich you, whatever the nibble.

Boundary signs

Sign and occupant(s) (Impressions)

Villages, towns, cities, counties and countries have boundary signs. Flowers displaying name, perhaps crest and the all-important 'Welcome' message often surround these signs. Whether it is places or people, first impressions count. What message(s) does our boundary sign give to those who meet us? Are we welcoming or hostile, accepting or judgemental, inward or outward-looking? Do people sense they are valued and celebrated, or at best, tolerated, at worst, rejected?

Boundary signs do not always reveal the true nature of their occupant(s). Unkempt boundary signs can mark the existence of loving communities. In contrast, polished signs might mark the presence of communities preoccupied with the shallowness of appearances. Likewise, some people have unattractive personalities, especially if battered by life, yet a beautiful gem lies within. Others might be whitewashed tombs, exhibiting surface charm and purity, yet dead within from selfishness. Is there perhaps a mixture of tomb and gem in all of us?

What message(s) do people receive from your boundary sign? Does your sign reflect who you are? More importantly, what is life like within yourself?

Twinning (Spiritual guidance)

'Twinning' appears to have originated post-World War II as a means of reconciliation. Roadside boundary signs often display the name of the place(s) with which they twin, known as friendship or partner towns or brother or sister cities. These twinning schemes testify to the value of developing a broader perspective on life through sharing ideas.

Twinning-friendship-partner-brother-sister has resonance in the spiritual life. It is a blessing to have help discerning what is happening in one's inner life. It might be a trained spiritual director, priest, counsellor, family member or friend. What matters is that the 'twinned person' helps you better understand the workings of God (Love) in your life. Spiritual guidance also comes from the Bible, Church teaching, spiritual books and spiritual exercises such as those of Ignatius of Loyola. Spiritual guidance brings perspective, a more objective view—height brings insight. Do you have a spiritual friend? Would you like one? Be ready to become a spiritual friend to another, but only *if* love asks this of you.

Follow the road ahead
(Spiritual guidance)

As a rule of thumb, when unsure of the way, it is better to keep to the road ahead rather than changing direction on vague hunches to turn left or right. In life, too, *sudden* changes in direction are seldom good. Unless life's traffic signs direct you otherwise, keep doing what you do. Carefully discern whether *love* is asking you to make a change.

In his fifth rule for discernment, Ignatius of Loyola teaches that when in spiritual desolation, without exception, we must not make any changes to previous decisions made when in spiritual consolation. In other words, when God seems far away (spiritual desolation), continue acting upon previous decisions made when God felt close (spiritual consolation). As Ignatius teaches, the evil one tries to lead us astray when we journey in love. Do not follow him; instead, '*Follow the road ahead!*'

Destination: Where are you going?
What are you doing?
(Morality)

You'll need your brain switched on for this—it gets tricky! Road directional signs have route numbers, e.g. A123 leading to Circle City. The same directional sign can also have route numbers in brackets, e.g. (B456) leading to Triangle Town. To reach Triangle Town, follow the A123, which takes you onto the B456. One's journey would be thus:

If you were travelling to Triangle Town on the above roads— *you know* what you are doing—travelling to Triangle Town. However, when you are on the A123, it may look to an observer as though you are travelling to Circle City.

There is an essential distinction in morality between ends and means. The 'means' is what you do (the act), while the 'ends' are why you do it (your goal). For example, you go to work (means) to pay the bills (end). In Catholic moral teaching, intended good consequences flowing from an intrinsically evil act (*an act always wrong in itself*) can never justify such an act. (*Catechism of the Catholic Church* 1753, hereafter *Catechism* and *CCC*) For example, you cannot justify robbing a bank (*evil* means) to pay the bills (*good* end). One issue within morality is that it is not always clear what someone is doing (i.e. the means/the act). The road analogy above involving Circle City and Triangle Town helps illustrate this difficulty. Where are you going? What are you doing?

When asked, "What are you doing?" a driver on the A123 could perhaps also speak truthfully by saying he is 'changing gear' or 'indicating' or 'steering'. Suppose one treats 'changing gear', 'indicating', and 'steering' as separate acts from the act of travelling to Triangle Town. In that case, logical consistency seems to require treating the travelling on the A123 in the direction of Circle City as a separate act from journeying to Triangle Town. On the other hand, suppose one treats 'changing gear', 'indicating', and 'steering' as *parts of the act* of travelling to Triangle Town. In that case, logical consistency seems to require treating the travelling on the A123 in the direction of Circle City as *part of the act* of travelling to Triangle Town. The challenge is distinguishing between 'parts of an act' from the 'act itself'.

In summary, our example appears to have at least three logical options: (i) Changing gear, indicating, steering, and travelling towards Circle City are all part of the one act of travelling to Triangle Town, (ii) Changing gear, indicating, steering, travelling towards Circle City are all separate acts from the act of travelling to Triangle Town, (iii) Find a more nuanced way to distinguish between 'parts of an act' and 'acts themselves'. Maybe one should speak of 'acts within a bigger act'.

The moral issue in all this is accurately identifying what one is doing. It is obvious most of the time; at other times, it is less so. Apply this insight to some examples in life: *What are you doing?*

Confirmatory signs
(Spiritual guidance)

As drivers, we might travel through a junction and question, 'Am I going the right way?' For some of us, it happens quite a lot! At such times, I am happy to catch sight of a confirmatory route sign that confirms the road number and destination. If one is on the wrong road, at least re-direction becomes possible.

'Am I going the right way?' moments also occur in the spiritual life. We always make decisions, some big, others small, and sometimes we are left wondering whether we have chosen wisely. With driving, as in life, preparation is key. The more we plan—before—making decisions, the less likely we are to take a wrong turn. After negotiating a life junction, what might our confirmatory signs be? They are unlikely to involve a visit from the Angel Gabriel, as did Mary, the mother of God, or being blinded and knocked off one's horse, as did St Paul. *Your* confirmatory signs will probably be a lot less dramatic. Perhaps so ordinary they are easy to overlook, similar to how you might *not* notice the beauty of dandelions in your garden.

Some people look for too many confirmatory signs. An analogy once given was of a driver hesitating to go at a green traffic light, motionlessly looking for a second or third green light before advancing. Healthy self-reflective doubt has, for sure, an essential place in the spiritual life—but when you sense it is time to act, have the courage to get on with it.

Opportunities may open up after you make a decision, which, rightly or wrongly, might boost one's belief that the direction pursued is correct. On the other hand, hardship and suffering may follow. These difficulties might suggest it is the wrong path—yet it is crucial not to simply equate trials and tribulations as a sign of an errant route. Look, for example, at the difficulties Mary and Joseph had in cooperating with God's plan of bringing salvation through Jesus Christ. Then, in the Garden of Gethsemane, Jesus' decision to do God's will led to His Passion and Death. Remember, the devil will seek to put hardships in the way of travelling the path of love. We, too, have our cross to carry.

A sense of rightness, an inner calm, is a good indicator of choosing wisely; one is on the correct path. Even then, have your spiritual wits about you. As St Paul reminds us, the evil one masquerades as an angel of light (2 *Cor* 11:14). Ultimately, inner confirmatory signs are rooted in one's trust in and loving relationship with God. The particular route(s) taken is sometimes less important than *how* we travel. When driving, several different roads can often lead to the same destination, even though some routes are more suitable than others. If we are on the right road, it will usually mean our personality, abilities, interests, needs and desires are a good match for the route pursued. Even when we are not on the *best* road, we can still find love, or more to the point, love can still find us.

What is *your* purpose in life? Are you pursuing the path of love? In your small and big decisions, what is love asking of you? 'Fall in love, stay in love, and it will decide everything.' (Attributed to Fr Pedro Arrupe, S.J. 1907—1991) What are the confirmatory signs of love in your life?

Road User

Road user interaction (Judging)

On the horizon, a roundabout awaits. Reading the road, you give way to the right and fit in with the traffic. Round you go, leaving by your chosen exit. Soon there are more junctions and traffic as everyone journeys on their chosen way. Interaction on roads is fleeting; we know little of the journeys of others. Some are weary, nearing the end of a long drive. Others are stressed as they struggle to find their way. Fresh-faced drivers change up the gears in hope.

We also encounter many people on the highway of life, sharing only fleeting moments. We know little, if anything, of their life's journey. How well do we interact? There is an old saying: good and excellent drivers make few mistakes, but only excellent drivers make allowances for the faults of others. Likewise, excellent people make allowances on the highway of life, seeking to understand and excuse rather than criticise and judge. Do you pursue excellence on the highway of life? As the eighteenth-century poet Alexander Pope said, 'To err is human; to forgive, divine.'

Road user unused (Unemployment)

When unemployed, society appears not to want you. You may be unemployed, but you are not broken down. Do not rust up—utilise yourself. Find a way to contribute to the world, no matter how small or humble it may seem. Unemployment is a life lesson; embrace the experience, reflect and learn from it. If *in* employment, especially high-powered and well-paid, beware of pride. Like a car crash, unemployment can hit when you least expect it. What matters is the inner journey and how *you* respond. Life employs everyone to love. You have a job for life.

Crashes
(Faults)

Rubbernecking. Do you do it? When driving past a road accident, some people morbidly stare at the misfortune of others. Similarly, there is an unhealthy fascination by some to gawp at the personal mistakes of people in the public eye. People love to throw stones!

No matter how much road users try to avoid them, crashes happen, some small, others big. There is no point in dwelling on a past crash if there wasn't anything you could have done to prevent it, but if *you* could have avoided the collision, there is a point— learn from it and move on. Journeying through life also involves inevitable crashes. In small and big ways, things go wrong. We collide with others, ourselves and God. In short, we fail to journey in love. What can we learn from our 'crash' moments? Were you or the other person at fault? Are you equally to blame? On the highway of life, even when it is the other 'driver's' fault, it is often better to let it go and move on—life's too short!

'Driving' attitude is a crucial factor in causing and preventing crashes on the road and the highway of life. How is *your* attitude? Are you careful and considerate? Do you take unnecessary risks? Do you get annoyed when 'people get in your way'? When others make mistakes, do you make allowances? Do you forgive or succumb to rage as you wonder why others are not as 'perfect as you'? We are all imperfect drivers.

Motorcyclists

Vulnerable and visible (Love)

'Think once, think twice, think bike' was the 1970's road safety campaign to reduce motorcyclist accidents at junctions. Reworked, it can also apply to how decisions in life affect others, especially the most vulnerable. Think once, think twice, *think love*.

Road safety campaigns also focus on being easily visible. Reflective clothing reflects light from other road users, helping to keep each other safe. Reflective clothing has a place in the spiritual life too. Reflective people affirm, praise and encourage, helping others recognise the goodness within themselves. In contrast, some people wear light-absorbing clothing. They criticise and blame; these sad souls are incapable of affirming others since it hurts their egos too much. Remember to wear that reflective jacket when you get up in the morning.

Pillion passenger (Trust)

There is the story of an older man comparing falling in love to holding the tail of a rocket. You don't know where you are going, but you know you must never let go. This wisdom also applies to 'riding pillion' in the spiritual life. If a motorbike is the rocket and you are the pillion passenger, the rider is love.

Christians ride with Jesus. Bike riding—with Jesus upfront—does not deny free will. You can choose not to get on the bike. If riding, you can tap on the rider's shoulder and get off—ride with someone else if you wish. But, if you *choose* to 'ride pillion' with Jesus, you must trust in the direction he is taking you and *hold on!* 'Riding pillion', however, is not passive; the rider and passenger work as a team. It involves being still, relaxing, and leaning with, not fighting against, the rider. In following divine love, Christians lean with Jesus as we travel the highway of life.

The purpose of the yellow road sign picturing a motorbike with the slogan, 'To die for . . . ?' is to promote road safety. However, it is worth dying *to sin* to ride pillion with Jesus upfront on the highway of life. 'I have been crucified with Christ; and it is no longer I who live, but it is Christ who lives in me. And the life

I now live in the flesh I live by faith in the Son of God, who loved me and gave himself for me.' (*Gal* 2: 19-20)

With whom are you spiritually riding? Do you know you must never let go, or do you sense you should be tapping *someone's* shoulder? 'To die for . . .?' You bet!

Crossing the road
(Vocation)

Those of us of a certain age will recall the introduction of the Green Cross Code in the early 1970s, a campaign to help people cross the road safely. Its six-part guidance was: 'Think, Stop, Look, Wait, Look and Listen Again, Arrive Alive'.

Discerning one's vocation has been described in terms of 'Stop-Look-Listen'. We need to pause, see what is going on in our inner lives and the world around us, and listen to how God invites us to respond in love. We must work out how *love calls us* in life's big and small decisions. There is a danger in crossing the road and stepping out on the highway of life, but we must move. To remain stationary is to become a bollard obstructing the path of love.

In what direction is love calling you? Think, stop, look, wait, look and listen again—but then cross the road! You will be journeying in the spirit of your maker, living a life of love. *Mind the kerb!*

Driver not passenger
(Decisions)

As a driver, one constantly makes decisions: turn left, right, or straight ahead. It is the same with life; we are not passengers, passive recipients of fate. Many things are beyond our control on the road and the highway of life, yet we can choose our response. We choose freedom by refusing to become puppets of limiting circumstances and constraining forces. One's attitude and response determine the person one becomes.

We must respond appropriately to the challenges of life, whatever the circumstances. How do you respond when another driver 'cuts you up'? How do you react when travelling behind a slow-moving vehicle? How do you react if others try to intimidate you off the road because you are 'in their way'? Your response can teach you about your character. Reflecting upon his experience as a prisoner in the Auschwitz Nazi concentration camp during the Second World War, Viktor E. Frankl in *Man's Search for Meaning*, champions the important truth that we are always free to choose how to respond to situations, and this can never be taken away from us.

Do you know The Serenity Prayer? 'God, grant me the serenity to accept the things I cannot change, the courage to change the things I can and the wisdom to know the difference.' In what areas of your life do you need serenity, courage, and wisdom? You are no passenger. How will *you* respond to *your* challenges?

Pedestrians

Children and rules (Conscience)

Because children learn by example, the Highway Code instructs adults out with children to always use the Green Cross Code in full.[2] What should adults do, one wonders, when not out with children? Are there justifiable exceptions to the Code? More importantly, how should we approach rule following in general?

The American psychologist Lawrence Kohlberg (1927-1987) identified six stages of moral development within three levels: pre-conventional (4-10 years), conventional (11-adult) and post-conventional (higher adult). The pre-conventional level is about following authority figures. As regards the conventional level (observing laws to maintain social order), Kohlberg said most adults reach this—but no further. Few, he thought, reached the moral maturity of the post-conventional level (adherence to universal moral principles absorbed into one's conscience, regardless of disapproval from others). 'When I was a child, I spoke like a child, I thought like a child, I reasoned like a child; when I became an adult, I put an end to childish ways.' (1 Cor 13:11) How adult are you? At which level might you be?

Children and ice cream (Attachments)

Children may unexpectedly run into the road when seeing an ice cream van. In life, adults act like children when grasping after things to the exclusion of a balanced and considered view of life and their place in it. Blind pursuit of possessions, power, status, and relationships rob people of inner harmony—*they lose love*. Is there any ice cream grabbing in your life? Is your pursuit of something or someone making you unloving to others, yourself, and God?

In his spiritual exercises, Ignatius of Loyola speaks of *indifference*, meaning choosing what leads to the love of God and neighbour and abandoning all that does not. It means focusing on being the person God has made you to be and living in harmony with His will. One thus becomes indifferent to both the favourable and unfavourable circumstances of life. By letting go of childish ice creams, we gain everything. We gain love.

Dog lovers, leads and drains (Fear)

I use an extendable lead with Joe, my beloved Jack Russell Terrier. He is a lead puller. His pace is not my pace; his ways are not my ways: tug, tug, and more tugs. Joe teaches me something about how God deals with us. For the protection and benefit of the impatient soul, I can imagine God using an invisible extendable lead. We thus learn to walk at God's pace and go in His direction. God will prompt us and encourage us, yet we remain free to tug, go elsewhere and chase the latest smell that catches our attention if we so wish.

Freedom from sin requires sensitivity to the master's promptings. If we pull too hard, God will respect our free will and let go of the lead. Then what? Simon Peter uttered, 'Lord, to whom can we go? You have the words of eternal life.' (*Jn* 6:68) Being genuinely free is, perhaps, a bit like being an unleashed dog spontaneously running in the joy of the present moment while attentive to his master's voice.

My dog, Joe, has a phobia of road drains. Maybe he once got his paw caught in one; I don't know, and he probably doesn't. An exaggerated reaction kicks in when he sees a drain, and Joe keeps a safe distance from the naughty black drain waiting to swallow him up! It is natural to experience fear. Some fears are rational (e.g. a tiger is running after you). In contrast, other fears are irrational (e.g. no, that one-centimetre spider will not kill you). *All* fear, nevertheless, is an obstacle to love (God). Worries, anxieties, panic attacks and phobias all boil down to fear. 'There is no fear in love, but perfect love casts out fear; for fear has to do with punishment, and whoever fears has not reached perfection in love. We love because he first loved us.' (1 John 4:18-19)

Your fears must not rule your life, whether tiger or spider. Have courage. 'Be still, and know that I am God!' (*Ps* 46:10) You do not walk alone.

Walkers (God's presence)

Walking is one of the most basic activities, yet so enriching, so divine. We might walk in the company of others or alone. Both social and solitude have their place. Do you doff your hat or don your mask? When meeting other walkers, some bury their head in a mobile phone. Others wear blinkers, staring straight ahead. Some look elsewhere at something that has 'suddenly caught their attention'. One way to deal with this is to fire a prayer or kind thought at on-coming walkers. If any mask-wearers walk past, offer another prayer/kind thought to help them on their way.

After the Resurrection, Jesus's disciples were walking on the road to Emmaus, and Jesus joined them. However, at first, they failed to recognise him (*Lk* 24:13-35). Jesus walks with you—be sure to notice him. God is both in your solitude and in your fellow travellers.

Runners (Present moment)

When walking, one foot is always on the ground. With running (including jogging), there are brief moments when both feet are off the ground. This float phase symbolises the present moment, the only existential reality, sandwiched between the past (one foot on the ground) and the future (the other foot on the ground). Although gravity ensures the float phase is brief, it's as if one were flying. The 'Flying Without Wings' song by pop band Westlife speaks of becoming complete by finding our special thing in the strangest places. Amazingly, life's truly special 'thing'—*God*—can be found in *every* present moment.

The present moment is a glimpse of eternity, a transcendence of time. Past and future do not exist in the present—they never have and never will. The past *used* to exist as a previous present. The future *may exist* as a future present, but only the present moment exists *now*. While the present makes sense within the context of what has gone before and lies ahead, 'past' and 'future' can distract us from living in the now.

God's uncreated eternal presence is surely both outside time and present within. Maybe this is why the present moment, our float phase, seems to offer a glimpse of eternity. Westlife's song also says I love you, anytime, anywhere. By learning to live in and love the present moment, we say 'I love you' to life's special 'thing', the *God of Love*, anytime, anywhere.

Projection markers
(Ego)

Red and white triangular projection markers are required for vehicles with *significant* overhanging loads to warn of potential danger. People's egos are like overhanging loads; tolerance exists if they stay within safe limits. Attach a metaphorical projection marker for dangerously oversized egos and allow plenty of room. John the Baptist said, 'He [God] must increase, but I must decrease.' (*Jn* 3:30) We move from sinner to saint by replacing selfishness with love. The only overhanging load Christians need to carry is a share in the Cross of Christ Crucified—projection markers are not required.

Lorries
(Awareness)

'How's My Driving?' signs on commercial vehicles are common nowadays. People report driving behaviour causing concern and hopefully praise good driving too. Various telematic devices also monitor driver behaviour, providing feedback to bosses and insurance companies. Feedback is all the rage. 'How Did We Do?' requests pester shoppers, educational managers analyse students' comments about teachers, while restaurants anxiously check customer reviews. Fair and constructive criticism is helpful, as well as affirmation and praise. Nowadays, however, we seem to be living in a chronic complainers' paradise.

How is *your* driving on the *highway of life*? The irony in our feedback-complaining culture is that many people are not interested in discovering how well they live. 'How's My *Living*?' sign! Now there's a thought. People are often deaf to the voice of God (Love) speaking in the silence of their hearts. God's feedback matters if you wish to drive better on the highway of life. What feedback is God sending you?

Crossroads (Decisions)

There are two ways to turn right at crossroads when an oncoming vehicle is also turning right: turn in front or behind each other. Turning behind is usually less problematic as both drivers maintain greater visibility. In life, when we have to make decisions that disagree with others, we should do it in the least problematic way. Why cross someone's path when you don't have to? If it is necessary to turn in front of someone, take care and make sure *you* follow *your* road.

Drivers

All in the mind (Attitude)

There is truth in the saying that the most dangerous part of a car is the nut behind the wheel. Attitude and attention are key factors affecting road safety and essential elements on life's highway. Love is more an attitude than a feeling. It is about how we relate to others, ourselves, and God. The more we accept God's unconditional love for us, the more we grow in love.

We have our likes and dislikes; we get on better with some than others. Nevertheless, our calling is to love *everyone*. St Thérèse of Lisieux disliked one of her fellow nuns, so she looked for ways to be kind to her. One day, that nun said, 'Sister Thérèse, tell me, why do you like me so much?' Let us follow the example of St Thérèse. Some say the person you like least in life is the one you will be next to in heaven. If that sounds more like hell than heaven, it is because we are still imperfect drivers, imperfect in love. Take heart—even St Thérèse had her 'driving' faults.

When you learnt to drive, were you aware of other learner drivers far more than you are now? Alternatively, when you were looking to buy a car, did you notice vehicles for sale in a way that no longer interests you? If neither applies to you, perhaps think of someone you know who has learnt to drive or bought a car. Selective attention refers to the things we focus on from the vast amount of data available. We sift out, ignore what is not important to us, and allow in and attend to what is.

We need to be selective with our focus on the highway of life, remembering that attitude affects attention. The more loving we are, the more we see the good in others; the more judgemental we are, the more we focus on their faults. There is the tale of showing people a black spot on a white canvas and asking what they see. 'Black spot' is the usual answer; few say 'a lot of white'. How easy it is to focus on the faults of others rather than their large amount of goodness. St Augustine of Hippo described evil as the *absence of good*. A classic analogy compares evil to a hole in fabric; the hole (evil) in itself does not exist, but a lack of fabric (goodness) exists. When we focus on the black spots of others, we do so from the hole in our goodness.

On the highway of life, we all have L-plates in love. Perfect drivers don't exist. Nevertheless, the nut behind the wheel *trying* to focus on the good in others while seeking to love unconditionally is a saint in the making.

Hats (Judging)

'Be wary of hat-wearing drivers!' Years ago, this applied to flat caps, Panama hats and Trilbies. Nowadays, it also applies to beanies, bobbles and baseball hats. A stereotype is a generalisation about a particular group, which may or may not be accurate. Even if hat-wearing drivers are more likely to drive dangerously (*'how'* presumably depends on the type of hat worn), there are exceptions at the individual level. Stereotyping can have negative connotations, yet it is only natural to generalise to process information and make decisions efficiently. What stereotypes do you use? The challenge is to see through the stereotype to the individual within. Whether driving or any other human activity, what matters is what goes on underneath 'the hat' of *every unique individual*.

Women (People)

Do you think women make better drivers than men? Stereotyping? Statistically, women have fewer accidents than men, so on that basis, women are safer drivers. Ouch, that hurt! In addition, men have more accidents at speed, though whether women are worse at parking is a matter of debate! Being male or female affects driving behaviour; it also affects how we function in life. Indeed, there is *some* truth in John Gray's book title, *'Men Are From Mars, Women Are From Venus'*. Over recent decades, significant work has been done to ensure greater equality between the sexes. However, concerns over equality should not prevent us from acknowledging and celebrating the differences between Martians and Venusians. Equality does not always have to mean sameness. Given the fabric of our dual-sexed humanity, it is hardly surprising when this *natural* difference affects the nature of our earthling society.

Out with the old, not so fast (Ageing)

For young people, passing the driving test significantly boosts their independence; at the other end of the spectrum, being too old to drive is a severe blow. With increasing age, things once easy become a struggle. A gradual loss of capabilities and increasing dependence is the emerging reality. Ageing can be a humbling time—yet good for the soul. Even the ablest must accept that they cannot drive their hearse.

The Highway Code says the reactions of older drivers may be slower than others, so make allowance for this. With age comes wisdom, at least that's the general idea, so hopefully, a slower reaction time is compensated for by greater insight on the road. In life, a slower reaction time is often desirable. Avoiding kneejerk reactions and offering measured responses are signs of experience. Older people often make allowances for those reacting too quickly on the highway of life. How are your reactions?

According to Socrates, the unexamined life is not worth living. Whether driving or living, we are prone, as the quip goes, to have one year's experience many times over if we don't reflect. Advanced drivers see themselves as learners. Self-aware of their faults, they strive to be better. Do you see yourself as a learner driver on life's highway? The saying, 'A saint is a sinner that keeps on trying', speaks to us all. Give that a measured response.

Taxis
(Money)

There are, no doubt, many excellent taxi drivers; nevertheless, they get lousy press overall. Possible driving faults include speeding and lacking consideration for other road users. Time is money, which is probably the dynamic leading some taxi drivers to drive poorly. It's the same in life. If money is the currency of one's life, everything and everyone has a price; their worth to you in pounds and pence. Do you think people get in your way? Let taxis remind you to make love, not money, the dynamic of your life.

Routes
(Patience)

Our way of doing things is not always in harmony with love—God's way (cf. *Is* 55:8-9). On a road journey, we usually choose the quickest route; this makes sense in the absence of reason(s) to do otherwise. This logic also applies to the journey of life. However, the God of love is all-knowing (omniscient), so he knows the *best* route for us. He might guide us into taking the long way to protect us—and from what we might never know.

> When Pharaoh let the people go, God did not lead them by way of the land of the Philistines, although that was nearer; for God thought, "If the people face war, they may change their minds and return to Egypt." So God led the people by the roundabout way of the wilderness toward the Red Sea. The Israelites went up out of the land of Egypt prepared for battle. (*Ex* 13:17-18)

Can you see when the God of love has taken you on the long route? Maybe he is nudging you now to be patient.

Motorway services
(Rest)

Motorway services are spaced at frequent intervals. Tiredness kills, so two hours of driving is the recommended maximum before taking a break. In life, insufficient rest also affects our ability to function properly. Find God in your rest.

Route finder
(Spiritual guidance)

What are you like at finding your way? At times, we all need directional help. I prefer using a map to modern-day technology. On one occasion, I reached for my trusted map. However, I didn't have my glasses with me; I could see the map but not read it. I looked around, but there was no one. What's more, I had no mobile phone. I was alone and lost.

When lost, it can mean we don't know where we are, or we don't know how to get to where we want to be—maybe both. A GPS route finder locates you and shows you the way. On the spiritual journey, we can also get lost, with no one to help except, that is, God. Our spiritual GPS is the God of love. Tell him you are lost; he will find you and show the way. Like GPS, God finds and helps us from right where we are. Do you use spiritual GPS? I do, and I now have a mobile phone too!

Satellite navigation (satnav)
(Spiritual guidance)

Satellite navigation sometimes gets it wrong and leads us along roads we should not go. We learn not to rely on satnav entirely; we apply common sense when finding our way (Do not link this reflection with the previous consideration 'Route Finder'. Our GPS God never gets it wrong.). In the spiritual life, like satellite navigation, we have external sources of guidance, such as family, friends and especially religion. Yet, it would be foolish and immature to rely on them to the exclusion of the inner direction within ourselves. Not following what you sincerely and thoughtfully believe is the correct path is as irrational as a driver choosing to travel in a direction he believes is wrong. But you must first pay careful attention! Where is your inner compass pointing? Your *true* self points you to God. Do you have the courage to follow it?

Diversion signs
(Trust)

Roads can have signs with black symbols on a yellow background to help drivers follow a particular route; sometimes, it's a necessary diversion. These basic signs, such as a square, diamond or triangle, effectively guide traffic along what might otherwise be confusing routes. In life, too, we have confusing roads, blocked roads and diversions. At such times, trusting in and following our fundamental beliefs and principles—our basic signs—are vital in ensuring we find our way. It may be a scripture passage, a wise saying or an image of the crucified/ risen Jesus. In your life, what basic signs can you trust and follow when the going gets tough?

Cyclists

Cameras (Judging)

Cycle and dash cameras are popular, one reason being to capture evidence of the driving faults of others. If not careful, one can also travel the highway of life with an invisible judgemental camera attached to one's head. Jesus tells us not to seek to remove the speck from our neighbour's eye while failing to deal with the log in our own (cf. *Mt* 7:3-5). Those with the worst eyesight cannot see themselves. Do you have a camera on your head? If so, turn it off occasionally, or better still, throw it away.

First and last ride (Temptation)

As a child, I rode my bicycle in the lane behind our family home. The roads were dangerous, so I was only allowed to cycle in that lane *up to the last garage*—but no further! Temptation strikes young. Adam and Eve ate from the tree; I rode *beyond that garage*. A street was at the end of the lane, beyond which another lane beckoned. Oh, what excitement there was in my whizzing onto the forbidden land!

I once returned a watch to the wife of a deceased person. She told me her husband had not been retired long. On the day he died, he left home on a cycle ride but never returned. Heart attack, I think it was. Nobody knows how much peddle time we have between our first and last ride. So ride on, make the most of your time, and notice *your* garages!

Overtaking (Faults)

Cycling makes you vulnerable. Having overtaken a cyclist, I stopped at the side of the road to deliver a parcel. The cyclist spoke to me before cycling past. Annoyed, he pointed out that it is difficult for a cyclist to pass a stationary vehicle on a busy road, so I should have held back behind him before stopping. He was right. I was wrong. I accepted his point, telling him I would remember this. Looking shocked and pleased by the reaction, he went on his way. We can so easily, without intending it, negatively affect others, especially the most vulnerable. When one's errors are pointed out, let us accept and learn from them.

Highway Code (Rules)

Cyclists, of course, are not perfect; indeed, far from it by the way some of them ride. For example, the Highway Code states that traffic signs, traffic light signals, and stop lines apply to cyclists and other traffic. Yet, many cyclists act as though these rules do not apply to them. Similarly, some people follow certain moral norms in life, while others do not think they apply.

The Highway Code is the official code in the UK and applies to *all* road users. Yet, *parts* of the Code only apply to certain road users, not others. For example, drivers, not cyclists, need to wear a seatbelt. By analogy, theists believe God's Code is the official code—the Highway Code for life. Yet, do *all* moral norms apply to *all* people in *all* circumstances? When and why might legitimate exceptions exist? In what ways might a more nuanced interpretation and application of some moral norms be possible without contravening the will of God? Jesus said, 'The sabbath [with its rules] was made for humankind, and not humankind for the sabbath'. (*Mk* 2:27) What do you think?

Tandem (Marriage)

The 'Daisy Bell' folk song speaks of two lovers joyfully riding a bicycle made for two. *'Daisy! Daisy!'* Er, okay. Have you ever ridden a tandem? A key challenge is deciding who is at the front and who is at the back. The nature of a tandem is for some*one* to do the steering. Like lovers on a tandem, marriage is a partnership of equals—both can wear the Lycra if you see what I mean. Yet, both tandem and marriage need someone to lead and someone in support for a pleasant journey.

Are you on life's precious tandem? If so, which seat do you occupy? Perhaps you and your partner swap seats. What is crucial is that whoever is riding the rear saddle also peddles—especially on the uphills—and looks in the same direction as, and leans with, the front rider. Without loving teamwork, the marriage tandem is little more than two unicycles in disguise. When God shares the journey, it matters not where one sits.

Buses

Stop the bus (God's presence)

Dark outside and in an unfamiliar city, I stared out of the bus window. Stop after stop went by; eventually, I realised I was heading in the wrong direction. Thankfully, my bus driver flagged down another bus. Grateful and humbled by the experience, I boarded anew. We can also find ourselves in unfamiliar places on the journey of life; there may be darkness and anxiety. We get lost. Jesus is our shepherd; he always looks for his lost sheep to put them back on the right path. Help is always available. Are you humble enough to ask for help? Often, our answer comes through others.

Wheels on the bus (Death)

The journey of life is like a bus journey; getting on—birth, getting off—death, life itself existing before and after our brief ride. Most will not know the closeness of *their* life's exit; the wheels stop, the bus journeying on without us. Time is short for those with many miles on the clock. In future mourning, will there be a recalling of missed opportunities to share a little more time on life's journey?

The unborn wait with their ticket to get on board. Will others make room? Will there be disabled access? Will the colour of skin, gender, or diminished potential mean that others refuse to let them on? In addition, some might ring the bell on their own life. In the worst cases, travellers push fellow travellers off.

You are still on the bus. When your exit stop arrives, I hope you can look back and see that you tried, albeit imperfectly, to make the most of your journey. A connecting bus awaits; the driver knows where you are going. In gratitude and humility, trust him. He will get you home. Be sure, though, to catch the right one!

Touring
(Pilgrimage)

Touring resonates with the existential truth that life is transient. Everything is changing—passing away. We end up as ash or worm food, leaving behind everything and everyone. The shortness of life need not cause despair; it can spur us to make the most of our time. As earthly nomads, we wake up in the laybys of life, each day an adventure in love. We are more camper van than a static caravan. As for your post-mortem pitch, the celestial campsite always has room for lovers.

2

HIGHWAYS

Hills
(Spiritual guidance)

On a journey, uphill and downhill are the norm. It is the same in the spiritual life. Ignatius of Loyola had much to say about spiritual slopes, in other words, consolation and desolation. Simply put (too simply), in consolation, we sense within ourselves God's closeness, and in desolation, God seems far away. Fr Mike Schmitz of Ascension Presents uses the analogy of pushing a boat on a shore to explain consolation (tide is in and easy to push), desolation (tide is out and hard to push, though the tide is visible) and the dark night of the soul (tide is out and hard to push, but the tide is nowhere to be seen).

Like road hills, neither consolation nor desolation lasts forever. Ignatius identified and discerned these movements within the soul (our heart) and how best to respond. When in consolation, our relationship with God is easy; God feels close. Ignatius advises that we make the most of it and humbly enjoy. Inevitably, we reach desolation. At these times, Ignatius says we are to take heart and persevere with our search for and love of God. The struggle strengthens our faith, hope and love. The grind of the up slopes leads to the ease of the down slopes, a repeating pattern on life's journey. Can you identify times of consolation and desolation in your spiritual life?

When experiencing changes in our spiritual life, it is worth remembering that, as Christians, we believe God is outside of time yet operates within it. As such, God sees the big picture. Aquinas sought to explain this with the metaphor of God at a height (think mountaintop) looking down on the road of time below. On the road, travellers only exist in the present moment, but the past, present, and future are as one for God. *We* experience consolation and desolation *within time*; God sees the big picture and, as St John Henry Newman reminds us, 'knows what He is about'. Our role is to trust God and seek His will as we drive the present moments of life's journey.

Road markings

White paint (Awareness)

White paint embellishes our roads. Road markings offer valuable information. How well do you notice them? Do you, for example, pay attention to hazard lines? By analogy, how observant are you of the white lines in your spiritual life? On the road, 'more white paint means more danger' is a good rule of thumb. Learn from the white paint in your spiritual life.

Cat's eyes (Discernment)

'Cat's eyes' or 'road studs'? Reportedly, the 'Cat's Eyes Removed' sign seen at roadworks offends some people because they think it involves animal torture. Yes, really! Do you know the significance of the different coloured *cat's eyes*? There are white, red, amber, green, green and yellow. Like white paint, cat's eyes improve road safety and are ubiquitous on our roads. Percy Shaw invented the cat's eye in 1933. While driving in night-time fog, he saw the reflection of his headlights (some say in the eyes of a real cat). His invention was advantageous during wartime blackouts and has been incredibly useful ever since. Apparently, the comedian Ken Dodd once suggested that Percy Shaw might have invented the pencil sharpener if the cat had been facing the other way!

Driving in night-time fog symbolises the human condition of struggling to find our way. The illumination of a cat's eye from *our headlights* represents our reasoning capacity to discover the good. Theists believe this search is the search for God. Roads now use *solar-powered* LED road studs (*cat's eyes!*). They offer much more visibility than the conventional type. This more excellent illumination symbolises how God's revelation through sacred scripture improves our knowledge of the good.

Our understanding of God is minuscule in the extreme. It is like one's vision in night-time fog, barely seeing the road ahead, let alone the vastness of the night sky. Both types of cat's eye have their part to play on the road. On the highway of life, both revelation and reason show the way to perfect love.

Roads

One and many (Holiness)

The Church refers to holiness as 'the main road onto which converge all the little paths that are particular vocations.' Holiness is striving to become all that God intends us to be, nothing more, nothing less. To do this, we, the creatures, need to connect with our creator. People have different ways of connecting with God.

For Christians, the message is clear: Jesus said, 'I am the vine, you are the branches. Those who abide in me and I in them bear much fruit, because apart from me you can do nothing.' (*Jn* 15: 5)

Our particular vocational path is the state of life we choose, whether marriage, priesthood, religious, or single. Combined with this is how we earn a living. However, we cannot always pursue the work we would like to do; life has a way of closing doors no matter how much one patiently knocks. The goal is to seek God's will—holiness in this and all things.

There are different types of roads, 'A' roads, 'B' roads and unclassified. There are different types of jobs, well-paid-high-status, low-paid-low-status, and unemployment; one might say these are the 'A', 'B' and unclassified roads of life. *All roads* are journeys into love if driven properly. It is better to be on a 'B' or unclassified road and travel it well than be on an 'A' road that does not make you holy.

Are you driving the tarmac in front of you the best you can? Holiness is everyone's vocation; learn to love the road you are on. Where it leads, let love decide!

Roman roads (Holiness)

The defining feature of Roman roads is their straightness. The legacy of Roman roads in the UK includes The Fosse Way linking Exeter to Lincoln, Watling Street connecting Dover to Wroxeter, and Ermine Street stretching from London to York. Direct routes were the name of the game. In the reign of Roman Emperor Tiberius, when Pontius Pilate was the Roman governor of Judaea, did John the Baptist preach 'a baptism of repentance for the forgiveness of sins'. (*Lk* 3:3) The Gospel of Luke describes John as the voice crying in the wilderness, telling us to 'Prepare the way of the Lord, make his paths straight.' (*Lk* 3:4) What diverts us from the direct route on the inner journey to God? What tendencies within ourselves resist love? Tendencies can become deviations. With God's help, strive to make your paths straight to the Lord of love. Direct routes—was, is and always will be—the name of the game.

Road debris (Toxicity)

Gary L. Thomas in *When To Walk Away: Finding Freedom From Toxic People*, says that based on biblical principles, we should not allow toxic people to intoxicate us. We should avoid them as much as possible since, like Jesus, we should not permit toxic people to hamper our service to God the Father. Using the example of road debris, he says that if a big object is in the way (e.g. a couch on the road), one has to deal with it. Still, for debris on the roadside, we would not stop but continue driving. Similarly, we ought to do the same with toxic people. Are there toxic people in your life? Do you *need* to deal with them? It might be better to 'drive on'.

Three B's: bends, bumps and blocks (Discernment)

Do you tend to speed? When driving, you should be able to stop in the distance you can see to be clear. This advice applies on bends, too, where visibility is limited, yet many motorists fail to reduce their speed accordingly. It is the same on the highway of life. We can find ourselves racing into the unknown instead of slowing down and taking time to reflect on the road ahead. Life has a certain pace—God's pace—and it is in our interest to live in harmony with it.

A journey is smooth and seemingly effortless when driving on a newly surfaced road. Enjoy and make the most of it. Bumpy roads lie over the horizon. Nobody likes driving over bumps, whether on the road or the highway of life, yet they are part of the journey. There is no need to look for bumps, but do not fear them either. It is the same in the spiritual life. Spiritual consolation and spiritual desolation are our smooth and bumpy roads.

Your road is blocked. Do you get angry or wait patiently? How we respond to roadblocks on the road and highway of life says a lot about our character and, for better or worse, shapes it too. Find God in your roadblocks! John Lennon's song 'Beautiful Boy' ('Darling Boy'), says what happens to us contrary to our plans—is life. True, but life is also the realisation of our plans *when* they accord with God's will. On the highway of life, blocks are challenges to overcome or signs that it is time to re-think. Neither quitting nor flogging a dead horse is desirable. Provided one responds to life's roadblocks as best one can in a spirit of love, then whatever the outcome, we are on the road to newness, love, and God. Others may not see it this way, but with spiritual eyes, you know. Open your spiritual eyes and see. Whatever the roadblocks in your life, God is with you.

Traffic calming (Self-control)

Road humps, chicanes and rumble devices slow traffic down. We need help to control our speed. We also need calming measures in the spiritual life—everyday life lived through spiritual eyes. Identify areas in your life (patterns) where you need to slow down, hold back a little, maybe a lot. Do you start new ventures or make significant changes without adequate thought? Are you quick to criticise? In conversation, do you need to listen more and talk less? The best communicators are those who listen.

Your overall pace of life may be too fast. Living at *what you feel* is ten mph under life's speed limit may be better for you. To help, try driving your car at ten mph below the road speed limit—though probably not a good idea on roads with speed limits of thirty mph or less. Do not be rushed if others toot because you are going too slowly for them. Maybe other people's 'toots' on the highway of life are causing your rushed approach to life (if you have one). Drive your car and yourself at your own proper pace— *you'll find God's pace.*

Where there are speeding patterns in your life, develop spiritual calming measures. Take a deep breath before speaking; if someone is annoying you, fire a prayer at them rather than judgement; pray about life-changing decisions *before* acting. Take your time and be open to God's will for your life; it is the way of love.

Road rules (Rules)

The Highway Code's rules and guidance can seem daunting, a mountain of regulations, adherence to, arguably, destroying the joy of driving. Yet the Code only seeks to improve and make journeys safer. Most of us probably follow most of the regulations most of the time.

Utilitarianism is about maximising happiness. In the nineteenth century, John Stuart Mill in *Utilitarianism,* taught that pursuing happiness embraces rules—we need them. Rules, he says, are based on humanity's received wisdom, 'landmarks' and 'direction posts' pointing the way to happiness. Mill compares rules to a sailor using a pre-prepared nautical almanack to guide. We, too, sail the sea of life with ethical guides based on humanity's shared experience of what works (most of the time) in ascertaining right from wrong. Yet the following of rules, says Mill, is not absolute. While cautious about making exceptions, he says we need to break a rule if, at times, adhering to it does not maximise happiness.

Happiness is to Mill, as safe driving is to the Highway Code, as love is to Christianity.

"Teacher, which commandment in the law is the greatest?" He [Jesus] said to him, "'You shall love the Lord your God with all your heart, and with all your soul, and with all your mind.' This is the greatest and first commandment. And a second is like it: 'You shall love your neighbour as yourself.' On these two commandments hang all the law and the prophets." (*Mt* 22:36-40)

In explaining his ethical theory of situation ethics, Joseph Fletcher in *Situation Ethics: The New Morality,* says that 'love is in the driving seat'. The most loving course of action, he instructs, is the path we should take, whether that involves following or breaking *any* rule. At *face value,* Fletcher's approach is reasonable; after all, God is Love, so an ethic based on the concept of love is undoubtedly good. The reality, however, is that it is not always clear what love requires. The Catholic Church points out that situation ethics denies God's will as revealed in the Bible and natural law. As such, *some—though certainly not all—*ethical rules are absolute (can never be broken) because these absolute rules protect human dignity. However, breaking an ethical rule *without damaging human dignity* can be justifiably broken if love is better served by so doing.

We are considering our relationship with rules. When a road sign informs drivers they have 'priority', oncoming traffic has an order sign telling them to give way. In addition, *not demanding* priority when it is yours is what excellent (loving) motorists do. In driving and life, it is better not to take what is ours when the most loving thing is relinquishing one's claim. If good rules reflect the minimum love expects, sacrificial love reveals the maximum love expects, the spirit behind good rules. Love embraces good rules and takes us beyond, like a motorist not insisting on his priority. Do you think of rules in terms of love? Are you a rule follower or a love follower? Rules and love often overlap; sometimes, they don't.

New roads (Change)

Driving the same old roads gets boring; we take our surroundings for granted and drive on automatic pilot. In contrast, driving new roads perks us up; we become more attentive. It is the same with life. We all need a change, a shake-up now and again to avoid falling into a rut, doing the same old. What new roads might bring you a new lease of life?

Following requests from his children to turn this, that or the other way, dad drove down roads to see where they went. One big adventure! What fun! Similarly, what fun it would be if we took a few mystery drives in life. If one is not abandoning responsibilities, changing and trying something new can be life-enhancing. Are you in need of a change? Life is an adventure. Might the mystery of love be inviting you to explore new roads?

Railway level crossing (Decisions)

When red lights show at a railway level crossing, one must not go beyond the stop line. A sounding alarm or lowering barrier also means no crossing. We also get metaphoric red lights, alarm bells, and barriers in life. These are when we clearly ought not to follow a particular path, desire, interest, curiosity or request. Only a fool would ignore such danger warnings. For example, others may ask you to do something you believe you should not do. Alarm bells, red lights and barriers are discerned within. Should others persist in their request, they do not respect *your* decision; metaphorically, they are tempting you onto the railway line. Keep your foot on the brake. Only *you* drive *your* car. Trust your intuition.

At other times, deciding how to proceed is more like dealing with an *open* railway-level crossing. There are no red lights, alarms or barriers, so one observes and proceeds cautiously. To get on with life, one has to make decisions. Furthermore, once you have decided to act, get on with it; you wouldn't stop halfway when crossing a railway line. How well do *you* make decisions?

Pedestrian crossings
(Rules)

Pelicans and puffins. These sound like the inhabitants of a nature reserve; they are, of course, the names of pedestrian crossings. PeLiCan (Pedestrian Light Controlled) crossings work to set timings. Sometimes traffic waits unnecessarily because the green man continues to display *after* pedestrians have crossed. PUFfin (Pedestrian User Friendly) crossings are a development of pelican crossings. They use sensors to ensure traffic only waits for as long as is necessary to allow pedestrians to cross. One might say the puffin crossing captures the spirit of the law behind the pelican crossing.

Even when no pedestrians are crossing, I do not advocate driving through pelican red traffic lights, since a casual disregard for traffic law damages road safety overall. It is good to ponder, nevertheless, that following the letter of a law, rule, or moral norm does not always capture the spirit behind the law, rule or norm in question. Can you think of examples of this on the highway of life? We need *moral* sensors to capture the spirit behind laws, rules and moral norms. What would Jesus do?

Motorways

Joining (Religious belief)

Zooming up the acceleration lane, one merges with an existing lane or enters a lane gain, the beginnings of a new motorway lane. Merging symbolises joining an existing belief system, while lane gain represents an additional avenue of belief. Nowadays, Christianity is more open to other faith traditions as viable ways to God; this does not, however, mean equanimity. Nevertheless, all traffic moving in the right direction is heading towards God, regardless of the lane.

When joining a stream of traffic, one needs the confidence to fit in. Others will often move over to help you. Likewise, in life, when joining a group, most people are welcoming, but you still need the confidence to fit in well. And, like joining a motorway, it is wise to stay in the left-hand lane for a while; blend into the traffic flow before considering overtaking.

Lanes (Discernment)

To be in the correct lane, one must pay attention to the signage. Some lanes are for one route only (e.g. M5), while others serve two or more routes (e.g. M5 & M42). Whether on the road or in life, it is often wise to keep options open if unsure of the *correct* way. Ultimately, of course, one *must commit* and get on with the journey.

Life is for love; how this works in practice can be unclear. We need to travel each section of life's highway a bit at a time, paying attention to the signage. Are *you* in the correct lane? Other than knowing your underpinning and ultimate destination is God, you do not need to know exactly where you are going on the highway of life. Learn to live with not knowing; let the mystery of life draw you on in love.

Someone once compared God's plan for our lives to a parent hoping his (or her) children would one day work for the family business. Some choose to; others do not. Those working outside the family business are not loved any less than those working for the business. Parents want the best for their children and know they must find *their* way in life. Similarly, God respects our choices. Your journey in love is not limited to one specific route. God's blueprint for you is dynamic, not static.

Nevertheless, it is wise to avoid sudden lane changes, both on the road and in life. Exceptions exist, such as avoiding a collision or one has a Road to Damascus moment. The rule of thumb is to chart a steady course and only make changes after careful deliberation—simple advice but often overlooked in the heat of the moment. When the going is tough, the temptation is to make a change. Life would be better if I lived elsewhere and had a new job, parish or partner. Would it? Most of the time—though not always—we simply need to change ourselves and our attitude within the lane we travel on life's highway. Pay attention to the signage.

Keep going (Well-being)

Motorways do not permit stopping or parking, except in emergencies. On the highway of life, when we are ill or facing a personal tragedy, life goes on with or without us, like the flow of motorway traffic. The Early Greek philosopher Heraclitus noted that one cannot step into the same river twice; everything moves on. Life *is* a life of change!

'Smart' motorways sometimes use the hard shoulder as a running lane. Many believe this compromises safety. Smart motorways may not be that smart. Likewise, overly pursuing gain can remove opportunities to get out of life's 'fast lane'. Excessively pursuing progress can endanger health and well-being. On the highway of life, the smart lanes are the hard shoulder for emergencies and laybys for rest.

Matrix signs (Trust)

Matrix signs can provide valuable advice and impose restrictions—though road users may not always be aware of the specific traffic conditions necessitating their use.[3] Matrix signs respond to traffic conditions. In life, we also need to watch for matrix signs within. We do this by getting more in touch with our true selves where God speaks.

On motorways, matrix signs might impose a temporary speed limit, tell us to change lanes or inform us that the road ahead is closed. When we don't understand the reasoning behind a restriction, we need to trust and follow it for our good and the good of other road users. On the highway of life, we only see the stretch of road we are on; God sees everything. 'For as the heavens are higher than the earth, so are my ways higher than your ways and my thoughts than your thoughts.' (*Is* 55:9) Do you trust the divine matrix, or do you think you know better?

Contraflow (Rules)

Contraflow allows traffic to cross the central reservation and drive the 'wrong' way. In the moral sphere, absolutists never cross the metaphoric barrier; non-absolutists see gaps in the central reservation. Absolutists on particular issues never permit exceptions, non-absolutists allow exceptions, often due to the circumstances within which a moral rule (norm) operates. Can you identify examples of disagreement between absolutists and non-absolutists? How does love fit into the issue(s) you are considering? When, if at all, might love require crossing the metaphoric central reservation?

Motorway junctions (Discernment)

Missing your exit means waiting until the next junction to make a change, which can sometimes involve a detour. In life, if we miss our opportunities, they may not come along again for quite a while, perhaps not at all. All we can do is wait for the next life junction and make the most of the road we are travelling. There is no going back!

Sometimes several motorway junctions lead to the same destination, one of them being the most direct. In life, even when we identify for ourselves an appropriate type of work, project or suitable lifestyle choice, our timing can be out—we may make our move too early or too late. Nevertheless, like motorway junctions, a less direct route can still take us to our destination. No matter the road, God knows how to get us back on track and travelling in the right direction. Trust Him and enjoy your journey.

Leaving (Death)

Motorways have direction signs one mile and a half a mile before exit junctions, and countdown markers at three, two and one hundred yards before deceleration lanes. Reaching one's exit should not be a surprise. On the highway of life, the signs at one mile and half a mile from our exit (death), not to mention the countdown markers, are often clear enough to see. Yet some people live as though they have not noticed them, thereby failing to prepare for their departure. Is it because they think life's exit junction is a dead end? Maybe they fear what might follow. Will you be ready when it's your time to leave this earthly highway of life? There is a time for everything. (*Ecc* 3:1-8)

Bridge

Basher (Ego)

When travelling under bridges, avoid being a bridge basher. A vehicle too high to pass is a metaphor for people with oversized egos. They cause problems for themselves and others. Who are the proud egotists in your life? How do you deal with them? Are you one? At times, there is a bit of a bridge basher in all of us. Are you humble enough to admit this?

Arch (Humility)

Regarding arch bridges, if there is not enough room, give way to oncoming vehicles using the middle of the road. Meeting oncoming vehicles is symbolic of human interaction, of *life!* Humble people know when one ought to give way; they do not need to hog the road.

Unseen (God's presence)

On a journey, we often pass over many bridges. There will be significant bridges—those we notice—but most of the time, we travel over 'insignificant' bridges—the ones we fail to see. Yet each bridge is vital to our journey. From the Christian viewpoint, God's grace (help) is always available to sustain us on life's journey. The trouble is that we sometimes fail to realise this, similar to those unseen bridges. God's love for us through the sacrifice of Jesus is the bridge of all bridges, yet this divine love often goes unnoticed and is denied by many.

Suspension (Fear)

While taking Joe, our beloved family Jack Russell Terrier, for a walk across a road suspension bridge, he was okay for a while, but panic set in. Afraid of the traffic and fearing falling off into the troubled water below, Joe needed reassurance. Little Joe conquered his fears and made the crossing. Joe resembles all of us as we make transitions of growth. We need courage and trust if we are to conquer our fears. What are the fears in your life that need conquering? Do you remember Simon and Garfunkel's song 'Bridge Over Troubled Water'? Jesus is the bridge over our troubled water.

Junctions

Why Stop? (Morality)

Stop and Give Way junctions are metaphors for the difference between absolute moral norms (i.e. always obey) and flexible moral norms (i.e. obedience depends upon the circumstances). To deny moral absolutes, some say, is the beginning of a slippery slope into moral chaos where, ultimately, anything, in principle, becomes justifiable. Logically, this is true; practically, it is not so straightforward. By analogy, one does not always have to stop at Give Way junctions. Yet, practically, you will *always* stop when it is unsafe to go—assuming you don't wish to cause harm.

An experienced driver negotiates unmarked junctions (no stop lines, no give-way lines) with extreme caution and uses his experience to drive them safely. Safety is to driving as love is to morality. Love is the ultimate guide for ethical decision-making. Moral absolutists (the Stop Signs) and moral non-absolutists (the Give Way signs) differ in their understanding of how love plays out in the realities of life.

Life also throws up new situations with no formulated specific moral norms—a bit like an unmarked junction. At such times, love guides the way. Down the road of time, some may concretize the application of love to deal with these types of situations by introducing new moral absolutes; others will not.

Virtuous driver (Virtues)

Driving experience, or lack of it, becomes most evident at roundabouts. With experience, what was once arduous is accomplished relatively easily and often unconsciously. Virtuous driving links to virtuous living.

Joseph Selling in *Reframing Catholic Theological Ethics*, offers the following explanation of a virtuous person's ethical reasoning. Most of the time the virtuous person makes decisions almost automatically 'in the blink of an eye'. Like the experienced driver, he is trained that way. Yet, says Selling, when an *experienced driver* deals with an unexpected factor, he takes more time to think. A virtuous person acts likewise when there is an ambiguity of circumstances and/or a conflict of rules. What are you like driving roundabouts? How well do you make ethical decisions?

Who's driving? (Free will)

Ethical decisions presuppose free will, the ability to choose one thing rather than another. We live as though we have free will (e.g. choosing to turn left or right at a junction), yet some people maintain that free will is an illusion.

C.S. Lewis in *Miracles,* pointed out that the worldview of naturalism (i.e. believing the world is nothing more than a physically interlocked system of cause and effect) leads logically to a denial of free will.[4] He argues that in a purely cause-and-effect world, 'decisions' are merely the effects of physical/material causes. As such, 'decision-making'—including choosing naturalism—is determined by cause and effect, not rational thought. Alternatively, suppose you believe humans have free will. In that case, you are logically committed to the worldview of supernaturalism (i.e. believing the physical world of cause and effect permits of non-physical elements too). Here is the key point: acceptance of free will leads logically to the possibility of and arguably is evidence for God. What do *you* think? Who drives your car?

Tactile paving
(Discernment)

To assist blind and partially sighted pedestrians, tactile paving uses raised surfaces that are felt underfoot. From a religious point of view, atheists and agnostics are spiritually blind. Furthermore, everyone is partially sighted. Humanity cannot grasp the divine mystery; at best, we merely glimpse the divine. Discerning God's will is an imperfect art.

In the fourth century, St Augustine said that man is *capax Dei* (open to God, capable of knowing Him). Some are better than others at knowing and loving God. Experts exist in most forms of life, so why not the spiritual life too? If one is ill, see a doctor. If the car is playing up, see a mechanic. If you need help in the spiritual life, see someone *correctly experienced* in spiritual matters. A priest or qualified spiritual director are the obvious ports of call for Christians. However, one can receive helpful Christian spiritual direction from anyone authentically sensitive to the workings of the Holy Spirit.

How will we know if we are hearing God correctly? Copper-bottomed guarantees are not on the table. Careful discernment with the help of *reliable* others is as good as it gets. The American Catholic Bishop Robert Barron once said that if you are doing spiritual direction on your own, the chances are your spiritual director is the devil. We need help to discern the workings of God properly in our life.

Spiritually sensitive people feel the tactile paving alerting us to God's warning and guidance. Many people, however, seem to wear thick-soled shoes, oblivious to the spiritual reality upon which they stand. The highway of life is uneven, and the devil tries to use this to lead us away from God. He also throws grit in our way to deceive us into thinking his ways are the tactile paving of our maker. Test the spirits and walk humbly with your God.

Signs, development of
(Morality)

Guideposts at parish crossroads became common in Britain following the General Turnpike Act of 1773. Known as 'fingerposts' because of their arm and hand shape with finger pointing the way, they are a valuable symbol for the moral and spiritual life. Moral norms (rules/guides), like fingerposts, point the way to desirable human behaviour (for theists, this is God's will). Human beings can also be signs pointing to God (Love).

To enhance road safety, traffic signs are designed to influence road users' behaviour. Likewise, Christian moral and spiritual teaching seeks to guide humanity towards God. Furthermore, traffic signage develops in response to our changing travel needs. Similarly, Christianity should evolve new ways to better apply the Good News to life's changing highway.

Signs, directional
(Ego)

A directional signpost, by definition, points away from itself. Similarly, the essence of a human being is to point not to oneself but to God. What makes us *truly* human is our ability to point to God. When a human being fails to be a SIGN of God's love, the 'G' (God) is missing, and consequently, the 'I' (me) becomes centre stage, as in the word 'SIN'. One cannot be a sign for God when pointing to oneself. Swiss theologian Hans Urs von Balthasar coined the terms 'ego-drama' and 'theo-drama'. Ego-drama: we live for ourselves with us in the staring role; theo-drama: we live for God whereby we accept whatever high or lowly roles God assigns to us. We point to ourselves when we live the ego-drama; we point to God when we live the theo-drama. In what direction are you pointing?

Signs and symbols
(False idols)

Traffic signs use symbols to communicate their messages efficiently and effectively. Christianity also uses images to help communicate the Christian message. Christian iconography dates back to at least the third century, while church stained glass windows date from the seventh.

During the Great Schism of 1054, when Eastern and Western Christianity split, icons were one area of controversy. Religious icons aid prayer, but some people worshipped the icon rather than what they represent. Modern-day readers are more familiar with icons on their mobile phones and other electronic devices. You use (go through) an icon to something else, perhaps a particular phone app such as Google Maps, a document, or the ability to phone or text.

The Greek word for 'icon' is *eikenai,* meaning 'to resemble', 'to be like'. Problems occur when people worship these icons rather than finding God through them. We shouldn't fascinate with phone app icons but use them to reach the 'real thing'. Likewise, the misuse of religious icons within Christianity was a failure to worship God through the icons. The same mistake happens when people worship nature, people and human artefacts.

Stained glass windows can also be misused. We might admire their colour, beauty, and artistry yet fail to discern the message. We can also think of ourselves as living stained glass windows. A stained glass window needs sunlight; no sunlight, no beauty and no artistic message. *We* are nothing unless God shines through. Without God, we point to the darkness of ego rather than allowing the divine light to shine. A sunbeam shining through stained glass sends its rays in many directions. Who knows the good effects we have on others when we allow the love of God to shine? Can people glimpse the divine light when they look at you?

Signs, types of
(Parenting)

Traffic signs make useful metaphors for understanding the parenting role within the family and the Church. Traffic signs fall into three basic types: inform, warn and give orders. Information signs are rectangular, warning signs are triangular, and order signs are circular.

Parents and families: Ordering, warning and informing all have their place. Orders lovingly given are a part of the discipline of younger children. Establishing boundaries and fostering responsibility is love in action. With teenagers, it's more to do with lovingly warning and informing. Parents of adult children inform (support) from the sideline with perhaps the occasional warning. Whatever the type of sign offered, one hopes the recipient latches onto the *value behind the sign.*

Church and human family: Ordering, warning and informing also have their place in the Church's loving care of humanity. I am speaking now of the *adult* children of God (i.e. adults and teenagers moving into adulthood). Although some may dislike order signs within the Church-human family relationship, non-negotiable Church teaching exists because of the Church's mandate to guide the faithful into the truth. The Church is only doing its job! When rejected, one hopes it is for a good cause and with a good heart. Rebelling without a good reason is juvenile.

Nevertheless, perhaps Church teaching requires a bit of repackaging. Suppose the Church communicated Christian values more by warning and informing and less by orders. Same values yet articulated differently. In that case, the human family might be more responsive.

Jean Heaton's blog 'Experiencing God's Love' on the Ignatian Spirituality website discusses false images of God acquired through upbringing. With sayings such as, 'God won't like it if you do that,' relatives and teachers gave her an image of God's love as transactional. Loved if one conforms; rebel and the love goes away. Alternatively, sayings such as, 'God won't like seeing you hurt yourself when you do that action' would have shone God's transforming and unconditional love. There is, perhaps, a lesson here for both parents and the Church. Maybe what *adult*-children of God need most is not so much order signs but informing signs and a few warning signs now and again. Having done that, leave the results to God.

What is your relationship like with your parents? What is your relationship like with your children? What is your relationship like with the Church? What is your relationship like with God? What is your relationship like with yourself?

Signs, informing
(Holiness)

You'll find them in pairs on narrow roads: rectangular information signs denoting priority and circular signs ordering traffic to give way. Some people are better at observing rectangles than circles, keen about their perceived 'rights' but not their responsibilities. In life, rights and responsibilities are often two sides of the same coin. In addition, narrow roads sometimes have signs informing of *passing* places; yet through selfishness or ignorance, some people park in them, causing problems for others. In life, selfishness and ignorance lead to taking what others need, most noticeable when others take from us, but less so when we take from others.

Signs can also inform of a no-through road (dead end) and a road unsuitable for motor vehicles. On the highway of life, what dead ends have you travelled down? Why did you go there? Did you turn around, or are you stuck? In life, have you gone down any unsuitable roads? Again, why was this? Was it a lack of self-knowledge? Did you not see the signs? Are you back on track? If not, why not?

Signs, warning

Two-way traffic (Life)

Two-way traffic reminds us that life is no one-way street. Not accepting different views from your own is like treating a two-way road as a one-way system—whatever goes in *your* direction. That is no way to drive, and it's no way to live.

Bends (Temptation)

Travelling along unfamiliar country roads from one county to another, I depended on bend warning signs. I was surprised at the seeming lack of uniformity between two adjoining counties; degrees of bend hitherto identified were now unmarked. It was unsettling for my driving. I needed to slow down, be more observant and take extra care. In time, I would have gotten used to these new roads. That journey reminds me of life as we move from the familiar to the unfamiliar. It might be a new area, new work, new relationships, new interests, new health problems, or new family issues. Whatever the change, it can be unsettling, *at least for a while.* Yet, if we take our time, pay greater attention and proceed cautiously, we find our way on life's unfamiliar roads.

Bend warning signs sometimes have an additional sign informing of an adverse camber. Adverse camber slopes away from the bend. Unless resisted, it 'throws' a vehicle away from the intended direction of travel. The driver experiences what *appears* to be a force drawing him outward from the bend (centrifugal force). Yet, in *reality,* he is experiencing a force keeping him on the intended direction of travel (centripetal force). A person observing the journey from *outside* the vehicle sees the centripetal force keeping the driver on track.

In the spiritual life, we can experience seemingly nothing but the lure of evil at times of temptation. Yet, within the struggle *against* temptation is the power of God, keeping us on the correct path. Like the observer outside the vehicle, it is often someone else who is best placed to see the centripetal force of God at work in our life when we cannot. All temptation is akin to driving road bends; each puts us at risk of going astray. There are many bends and many temptations, some big, others small. In his fourteenth rule of discernment, Ignatius of Loyola describes the enemy of human nature (the devil) in terms of a military leader attacking *his* enemy (i.e. us) at *our* weakest point. The weak spots in our character are perhaps where we are most likely to be 'thrown' off course; they are the *adverse cambers of our spiritual life.*

God is the centre of rotation around every bend. The more we anchor into our authentic true selves, the more we experience the centripetal love of God. As Ignatius says, when we find and follow what we *truly* want, we find and follow what God wants too. How well do you drive the bends on the highway of life?

Try your brakes (Self-control)

Before descending a steep hill, check whether you can control your speed and, if necessary, stop. In life, when at risk of being carried away with something, maybe work, an interest, a project or an idea, it is wise to check whether we can control ourselves. In addition, 'Try your brakes' signs sometimes come with an 'escape lane ahead' sign. This a reminder that life can get out of control, and we need to pause to regain focus. On the highway of life, do you need to try your brakes? Are you in need of an escape lane?

Falling rocks (Present moment)

The weather, another element of nature, or a climber might cause rocks to fall. On the highway of life, rocks can get in our way, obstacles on the journey of love. Events in nature are not evil. Still, they can challenge love, some even threatening our existence. The abuse of human free will is evil. In addition, humans cause suffering by accident, without malice present. By analogy, a rock climber unintentionally unseating a few rocks is quite different from one intentionally throwing rocks into the path of others.

You are a climber on the rock face of life, and *your* perch is the present moment. Below is the past, and above is the future. Your perch makes sense in the context of the entire rock face—but stop looking down! Furthermore, despite your plan of ascent—the present moment is the only part of the rock face life is asking you to climb. Where is your focus? Climb properly, and fewer rocks will fall.

Hidden dip (Awareness)

Have you driven a stretch of road with a hidden dip? You probably failed to notice the hidden dip if you didn't see the warning sign. These dips are called dead ground because hazards could be in the dip and out of sight until the last second. On the highway of life, our desire to get from A to B can sometimes diminish our awareness of the 'road' scene. We overlook hazards. Who or what might be the warning signs of hidden dips in your life?

Watercourse (Satan)

A roadside watercourse symbolises the saying that the stream of life runs alongside every moment. Finding the positives in every situation captures something of this spiritual awareness. Oddly, I once encountered a roadside watercourse where the water appeared to flow *uphill*. It was a gravity hill. They are more common than you might think and can give the appearance of such things as balls and even cars freely rolling *uphill*. The optical illusion involves false horizon lines in the surrounding landscape. It can easily deceive.

St Paul says, 'Satan disguises himself as an angel of light'. (2 *Cor* 11:14) Satan is very cunning. To lure people away from the truth, he masquerades as light. Yet, like gravity hills, what he offers is an illusion. Be warned! Satan (and his demons) create a false horizon and provide a false perspective. God is the only true horizon offering an accurate perception of reality. In one's search for God, Satan will be present too. He is the deceiver par excellence. Discern the spirits if you wish to discern the stream of life.

Tunnel (Gratitude)

The next time you drive through a tunnel, spare a thought for those who built it. Appreciation for their hard work makes one grateful. So often in life, we benefit from the efforts of others. Tunnels are dug in the spiritual life too. We encounter problems and need to excavate, sometimes very deep, to progress. It may be easier to go around an obstacle or remain on the surface, but avoiding problems and living shallowly will not foster love. Like the tunnel builders of past times, you may not live long enough to see the light at the end of *all* your tunnels. Yet rest assured, your effort and hard work in love are never lost. Those that come after will reap the benefits, like you, as you drive through tunnels made by others.

Signs, ordering

Clearway signs (Patience)

In life, it can sometimes be unsafe to stop what you are doing even though you may wish to. Like on the road, you have to wait until the clearway has passed. Be patient—nothing lasts forever.

Exception plates (Rules)

Occasionally, order signs come with exception plates added. Most order signs don't have exception plates, so no exceptions are allowed. In the moral life, justified exceptions to moral norms (rules) exist, yet how easy it is for human nature to make *unjustified* exceptions for oneself.

The 'Sort My Sign' campaign seeks to report unclear road signs, such as signs covered by overhanging tree branches and where parts of signs are missing. Unclear road signs are confusing, unfair and potentially dangerous. Similarly, it is also confusing, unfair and potentially dangerous when moral norms are ambiguous. Can you think of any? Are moral norms always clear to you? Unclear moral norms can sometimes lead to the mistaken need for an exception. Maybe we also need a campaign for the reporting of unclear moral norms.

Speed

Speeder? (Sin)

A driver's tendency to speed is akin to the human propensity to sin. Can you recall driving past a speed camera and thinking: 'Was I speeding? Did the camera get me?' At the end of a journey, if you wonder whether a speeding fine will soon pop through the letterbox, you know what I mean. Thinking like this destroys the joy of driving. Similarly, thinking the wrong way about mistakes (sins) on life's highway destroys the joy of living. *God gets the lot*, but He is not an over-zealous police officer set on prosecuting.

William A. Barry S.J. in *Praying the Truth: Deepening Your Friendship with God through Honest Prayer*, speaks of 'ungodly remembrance' and 'godly remembrance' (pp. 113—116). The former leads to 'darkness and despair', and the latter leads 'to turn ourselves away from self-destruction and towards a more abundant life'. Fr Barry says our past matters to God only 'because it affects the present and the future. . . . God's interest in the past is for the sake of transformation, of a change of heart in the present so that more of the future will be affected positively.' God wants us to learn from the past so we can have life to the full.

Rather than fretting over speeding and speed cameras, reflect upon why you might speed. You may need to allow more time for journeys. The point is to notice patterns in your flawed driving and do something about it. Take the same approach with life. Rather than obsessing over sins, look for your patterns of destructive behaviour and work with God (your friendly driving instructor) to drive better on the highway of life. *Mea culpa* (my fault)—yes; *damnata* (condemned)—no.

Speed cameras (Rules)

Friend or foe? While none of us wants a speeding ticket, most accept the need for regulating driver behaviour. Speed cameras exist for the good of society and its citizens—including you and me. Speed limits, their enforcement and the use of cameras provide a helpful analogy for reflecting on rules in general and our response to them. So, why do people tend to observe the speed limit when a camera is in sight? Is it out of self-interest or because speeding can affect others? Maybe it's a little bit of both. Now ask yourself why you follow any rule, law or norm, whether from civil authority, religion, or social consensus.

Suppose avoiding negative consequences to oneself is your only motivating factor for being lawful (i.e. following a rule, law or norm). In that case, you will probably break the law if you can get away with it. Alternatively, appreciating the value behind a law makes one far more likely to follow it—even though you may still find yourself pushing the boundaries! Do you perhaps keep to the speed limit *or thereabouts*, following the spirit, not the letter of the law? Does that ring true for you, *at least sometimes?*

Speed limits (Conscience)

The Bible, Christianity, Catholicism (Catholic Christianity), and presumably all religions have rules, laws and norms. How do you respond to them? Chances are, if you've left organised religion, their regulations and your response to them have something to do with your departure. Everyone has issues with aspects of organised religion, including, no doubt, the Pope. Jesus had a few too! The Catholic Church does not claim to be perfect. It is very aware of the corruption of sin within its own body (its members). Yet, it is also self-aware of the holiness and means of redemption at its very core—*God incarnate in Jesus Christ.* The Church is not perfect, and neither are its rules. As Catholic Christians, we seek God's will (Love) in and through this imperfect Church. The Church remains our best guide for regulating driver behaviour on the highway of life.

Whereas speed limits are generally not optional, Church teaching has nuance. Some Church teaching (rules/laws/norms) requires absolute adherence, while others do not. Nevertheless, the Church expects its members to adhere to *all* its teaching unless there is a powerful reason not to. Why? By analogy, consider mandatory speed limits and advisory speed limits. It is usually best for a driver to adhere to both types of speed limit since the Highways Agency offers this advice for our benefit, not harm. Similarly, the Church offers *all* its teaching for our good too.

Individuals in *good* conscience can sometimes disagree with Church teaching. That is not to say one merely has a difference of opinion. It means an individual has taken all reasonable measures to inform oneself and remains sincerely convinced that the Church is in error on a particular matter. At these and all other times, one has a duty to oneself to follow the light of conscience *even if it is in error—* of course, the sincere person, in error or not, believes he is correct. Think of your response to Church teaching in terms of speed limits. If you drive the highway of life trying your best to follow the Spirit of God's law, even if you notch up a few ecclesial speeding tickets, I am sure the film footage will be pleasing when your life is reviewed.

Average speed cameras (Virtues)

These little beauties record speed over a given distance to deter drivers from slowing down when approaching a camera and speeding up afterwards. Drivers slowing down and speeding up have yet to embrace the value behind speed restrictions. Average speed cameras are fairer because an otherwise good driver who speeds momentarily is unlikely to incur punishment if the rest of the drive is okay. If you struggle to view God as a friendly speed camera, at the very least, try thinking of God as the *average*-speed type. On the highway of life, a person fundamentally orientated towards God is unlikely to slow down approaching divine speed cameras and speed up after that. The former American basketball player and coach, John Wooden, had it right when he said, 'The true test of a man's character is what he does when no one is watching.' Of course, God is always watching—but lovingly.

Roundabouts
(Decisions)

One must pay attention to traffic signs and lane markings to select the correct lane when approaching a roundabout. Similarly, being in the correct lane in life requires *spiritual* awareness and acting upon the information available. Life is a series of decisions, interlinked (ideally) into a coherent whole. You have to make decisions at roundabouts; if not, you go nowhere except round in circles. Our present moments are like roundabouts; decisions determine the exit road from the present to the future. Life goes on, roundabout after roundabout. Although it is possible to go full circle at a roundabout, roundabout directional signs do not display a full circle. There is always a gap at the five o'clock position, a reminder that we cannot turn back the hands of time. The road from the present leads to the future, not the past.

Parking

Parking aid (Ego)

Are men better at parking than women? What is your *unbiased* view? Depending upon which survey you consult, data exists to support both viewpoints. A man (Dr Tony Heyes) invented the parking sensor (If he was married, maybe he designed it for his wife!). Whatever the reality, it is likely that men rate themselves better at parking.

Driving a long journey, passengers might sleep. Some wake up upon entering a car park and feel the need to find a parking space—as if you, the driver, were incapable of finding one. Perhaps one should smile and view it as teamwork. However, in life, some tend to let others do the hard work, only showing up when it is time to reap the benefits. How might one find God in these situations?

Car parks (Decisions)

When there are many vacant spaces, do you sometimes find you can't decide where to park? In life, too many options can also make it difficult to make up one's mind. Having fewer options is often a blessing. In these situations, find God by making the best of the spaces available.

King Richard III (Death)

In a Leicester car park in 2012, archaeologists discovered the remains of fifteenth-century King Richard III. Have you thought about your resting place? Not which graveyard, I mean the metaphoric car park in the sky. Jesus said: "Do not let your hearts be troubled. Believe in God, believe also in me. In my Father's house there are many dwelling places. If it were not so, would I have told you that I go to prepare a place for you?" (*Jn* 14:1-2)

I do not envisage competing for a heavenly parking space; my space, like yours and everyone else's, has our name on it. Provided we are our true selves, we will find our space. Park the front end in; you will not want to go anywhere else.

3

DRIVING

Car respect
(People)

We need to treat cars with respect if they are to perform well.
Respecting the dignity of every human person is also crucial to *our*
performing well. Whenever there is disharmony within ourselves,
families, communities, nations or globally, there is probably a
lack of respect for the individual somewhere in the mess. Despite
differences in belief regarding the implications of human dignity,
a shared concern exists when disagreement involves dialogue and
debate. Christians believe our lives are not our own; they belong
to God for the glorification of God (1 *Cor* 6:19). Christians believe
humanity's dignity is fundamentally rooted in its relationship
with God. We are *all* made in the image and likeness of God (*Gn*
1:27). That includes you. Respect yourself.

Consideration
(Life)

In many ways, how you drive reflects how you live. The Highway Code tells us to be considerate towards all road users, be understanding, and be patient. This is also good advice for the highway of life. Identify times in your life when you *received* consideration, understanding and patience. Identify times when you *gave* these qualities to others. The Golden Rule of treating others as we wish to be treated applies to the road and the highway of life.

Stalling
(Trust)

Stalling is a big issue for new drivers, yet rarely for experienced drivers. Two causes of stalling are a lack of power and applying power too quickly to the wheels. We can stall on the highway of life too. To help avoid stalling, draw strength from God rather than yourself and seek God's timing. A learner driver trusts his driving instructor. With effort and corrected practice, stalling rarely becomes an issue. On the highway of life, will you trust and listen to the divine driving instructor?

Cockpit drill
(God's presence)

Do you remember the cockpit drill? Door-Seat-Steering-Seatbelt-Mirrors (DSSSM). Do you still do it, or have you slipped into bad habits, such as adjusting the mirrors and moving the seat *after* the car moves? We also need a cockpit drill for the highway of life. Do you start your day peacefully, seeking love? It is about getting one's head and heart in the right place. For theists, it is about grounding oneself in God's presence and committing to staying in this place of trust throughout the day. Mother Teresa gave this advice: if you want a relationship with Jesus, begin your day by saying, "Good morning Jesus". What's your cockpit drill?

Decisions
(Conscience)

Decisions, decisions, decisions. You can't get away from them, whether driving or just living. Even deciding not to decide is a decision! Robots we are not; decision-making machines we are. To misquote Shakespeare's Hamlet, "To do, or not to do, that is the question." In the moral sphere, doing or not doing is a matter of conscience.

In Hamlet's soliloquy, he also says, "Thus conscience doth make cowards of us all . . ." Be that as it may *or may not be*, our actions flowing from our decisions doth make us who we are. As the *Catechism* teaches, when acting deliberately we are, in a way, the father of our acts. (CCC 1749) There is a self-reflective nature in what we choose to do.

Conscience doth make *moral heroes* of us too. God loves everyone unconditionally. We are all loved sinners; what we do or don't do in response to this truth is *the* question of life. Decision time!

Travel guide
(Saints)

Imagine going on a journey to a new place. Sure, you want to discover as you go, but that does not rule out consulting others. Only a fool travels without listening to anybody except himself.

On the journey of life, our parents are our first travel guides. Although life is a mystery, the journey into and through adulthood is not a mystery tour. In addition to our inner compass, the Bible and Church teachings are our travel guides par excellence. Furthermore, many fellow pilgrims have already been there, done it and got the T-shirt. While everyone has a unique pilgrimage, in reading the lives of the saints, we learn from those who have successfully travelled the inner spiritual journey. Through God's grace, many saints who once lost found their way.

Do you feel drawn to any saints? They'll make excellent travel guides for you. If you don't know of any, do some saintly research. Don't try to be them—be yourself, but learn from their experiences. Everyone's fundamental purpose in life is to be a saint. Saint *You!* Saints are happy in their souls. The road to sainthood is found by striving to live moment by moment with and for God. Your journey to sainthood starts now, not tomorrow or yesterday. *Now!* Get on with it. Ask God to make you a saint.

Reversing (Memories)

The Highway Code tells us we must only reverse as much as necessary. We reverse to make progress. We might reverse to manoeuvre into a space or turn around because we missed a turning. In life, too, we should backtrack only as much as necessary. Only look back to make progress *in love*. Look back to live, not live to look back. 'No one who puts a hand to the plow and looks back is fit for the kingdom of God.' (*Lk* 9:62) The windscreen, not the back window, is the main field of vision. Where is your focus?

Locked out
(God's presence)

Have you ever locked yourself out of the car? Where's the key? Far worse, have you ever felt locked out of your soul? By that, I mean not being in touch with your true self; you feel off-centre and that all is not well.

In searching for a car key, it is helpful to retrace one's steps. Who, what, where, when, and why did the key go astray? Take a similar approach if the key to your soul goes missing.

God will reveal the lost key to your soul—*if you are prepared to listen!* Jesus wants you to start this journey and allow him to love you. The door opens, the engine starts, and you are on your way.

Fuel—low
(Rest)

Are you one of those who let the needle hover by the empty yet persist in driving a bit more? Driving with low fuel risks running out in traffic, causing danger to others and yourself. In addition, contamination can dredge from tank settlement. Likewise, there is the temptation (not suffered by everybody) to push oneself too much on the highway of life. Lack of sleep and relaxation makes one too tired to meet life's demands. When tired, the mind is also more at risk of contamination by negative thought patterns.

I once ran out of fuel when giving a colleague a lift from work. I knew the fuel was low, probably only enough to get home, but I took the risk and suffered the consequences. While going the extra mile in life is good, we also need to know when to say "No". On the highway of life, don't ignore the warning light when your fuel is low. Find a way to get the rest, break or holiday you need. God is in your neighbour in need but also in *your* warning light. There was no virtue in my running out of fuel when giving my work colleague a lift. At the time, we both worked at a petrol station. God is, indeed, right in front of us (See Brian Grogan S.J., *God Is Right In Front Of You*).

Traffic lights

Temporary (Patience)

Temporary traffic lights are a nuisance when we are keen to get somewhere. They can also be a blessing in disguise, offering time to pause and reflect a little and, of course, who knows the dangers we have avoided by being held up. On the highway of life, we can expect God to put temporary traffic lights in our way if it is in our best interests. Where are the temporary traffic lights in your life?

Broken (Trust)

You can't stay at broken traffic lights forever; eventually, you have to make a move. Similarly, on the highway of life, we want reassurance that it's okay to go, but sometimes confirmation seems lacking, yet we know we have to choose. At such times, we act in faith, do what appears right and trust in God's providence. Vinita Hampton Wright in 'Four Principles of Pilgrimage', notes that similar to how a stationary car cannot be steered, God cannot guide us unless we have the courage to move.[5] On the highway of life, when necessary, do you have enough faith to drive through a 'broken' traffic light?

Driving

Sunshine (Sin)

Driving in sunlight shows up scratches and dirt we tend to overlook. This awakening might inspire one to reach for the sponge, bucket and polish, though most of us don't bother. In the spiritual life, the light of God shows up our imperfections. Can we be bothered to respond? God does not reveal our flaws to make us feel bad. He encourages us to rid ourselves of whatever hampers our reflecting the divine sunlight back to God and our fellow pilgrims.

How aware are you of the scratches and dirt in your life? Ask God to shine his sunlight on you. When He does, like Ignatius of Loyola, see yourself as a *loved* sinner. You will be happy and hopeful, your days filled with joy. If it makes you unhappy, despairing and sad, you only see yourself as a sinner. Remember, *you* are a *loved* sinner. Grasp that, and your life will change for the better. Perfect love is shining on you.

Awareness (Present moment)

While planning ahead and using the mirrors are essential to good driving, the only bit of road we drive is the tarmac under the wheels. On the highway of life, we only exist on the tarmac of the present moment. Intrinsic to the present moment is the context of the past ('previous present' moments) and the future ('future present' moments), yet, the present moment is all that exists.

Eckhart Tolle in *The Power of Now: A Guide to Spiritual Enlightenment*, talks a great deal about the present moment. He makes the distinction between psychological time and clock time. Psychological time refers to the human tendency to dwell in the past and reach into the future, thereby failing to be fully present in the present—the only moment there is. Tolle refers to psychological time as memory traces and anticipations. Clock time is the sequential ordering of present moments that is life itself. Tolle's point is simple yet profound and not, of course, unique to him.

Using the mirrors and scanning the road ahead is analogous to reflecting on the past and planning for the future. However, this can unwittingly give a false impression that roads once travelled and roads to come—exist. They don't. The road behind disappeared the moment you left it. Your road ahead will only exist if and when you drive it. 'Psychological time', as the name suggests, only exists in your psyche, your head! Psychological time is neither past present moments nor future present moments.

Safe driving requires planning and frequent use of mirrors. Happy living requires focussing on the tarmac of the present moment. The future and the past are the necessary non-existent contexts of the present moment. St Augustine of Hippo prayed, "Trust the past to God's mercy, the present to God's love and the future to God's providence." How aware are you of the present moment? The time is now.

Mishandling (Well-being)

Some cars are more robust than others but treat any car poorly, and it soon wears out. Wear and tear take their toll. Yet, regardless of registration date and miles on the clock, if cared for, a car will serve you well. Don't, however, exceed its capabilities. Nurse your car if need be. It's the same with us. Regardless of your registration date and miles on the clock, look after yourself and keep chugging along, accepting your limitations. Know thyself.

Accelerating
(Self-control)

How quickly can your car accelerate? Is it important? Drivers are a mixed bunch in their approach to speed. Most aren't interested in how fast their car goes, while some are heavy on the gas pedal. How about you?

Learner drivers often accelerate towards hazards they have not seen, the instructor's foot hovering over the brake. A prompt or two may do the trick. On the highway of life, experience often sees hazards inexperience does not. Listen for the prompts alerting you to danger and the need to slow down. Rush, rush, but to what?

Braking?
(Morality)

The friction heat caused by depressing the brake pedal evaporates water on the brakes. It is not always easy to know what someone is doing. For example, is one braking to dry the brakes or drying the brakes, which causes the car to slow down? It may be a case of pressing the brake pedal, causing the brakes to dry and the car to slow down. The moral analysis of human action can be a bit of a puzzle. What do you think the driver is doing in the above 'brake' scenario? God knows what the driver is doing, even if others might not. God knows us better than we know ourselves.

Gear changing
(Life)

How smooth is your gear changing? Do you and your fellow travellers get a bumpy ride? Likewise, do you make smooth transitions on the highway of life, or do you jump change and make life unnecessarily awkward? Pausing the foot before taking it off the clutch helps avoid rough gear changes. Similarly, pausing to reflect before making transitions helps foster more harmonious life changes.

In addition, heavy-handedness is not conducive to good gear changing. Hold the gearstick firmly but gently. Hold life's opportunities firmly but gently too. Tilting one's hand towards the desired gear helps good gear changing; correctly done, the new gear falls into place. In life, offer oneself up to the gateway of change—but don't force it.

Coasting
(Love)

Coasting means a vehicle moves while the engine is disconnected from the wheels. It can occur when a car is in neutral, or in gear with the clutch depressed. In life, people coast too. Coasting in neutral is having a free ride at someone else's expense. Not fully applying yourself is like coasting with the clutch down. Love pulls its weight. Any coasting in your life?

Breakdown

Free recovery, await rescue (Failure)

Have you ever broken down in your car? If not, your time will surely come. Imagine breaking down without a mobile phone and no one to help—you are helpless. You need to get going again but can't fix the problem yourself. You then realise you are within a roadworks area. You notice a sign saying 'Free recovery, await rescue'. "Thank God for that!" you may well cry, whether or not you believe in God. In life, there are human breakdowns; our wheels stop turning for one reason or another. Yes, God helps those who help themselves, but sometimes asking for help is all we can manage. We may need a spiritual mechanic.

Life is for love. It's that simple. If you've broken down on the highway of life, you've broken down in love. Theists believe God is love. We are to accept God's unconditional love for us and love in return. 'We love because he [God] first loved us.' (1 *Jn* 4:19) Get that, and you'll be happy! If you've broken down on the highway of life, ask yourself two questions: Am I allowing God to love me? How should I respond to this love? Keep asking those questions, and your spiritual wheels will start turning again. Thankfully, life's journey from the cradle to the grave is the roadwork of love. 'Free recovery, await rescue.'

Good Samaritan (Love)

The story of the Good Samaritan teaches us to help our neighbours, including our enemies, those who do not love us (*Lk* 10: 25-37). I once passed a broken-down vehicle while its 'driver' waved at the other passing motorists and me. In the mirror, her look of disgust was plain to see. We weren't bad Samaritans; it was neither clear there was a problem nor was it safe to stop.

Some people are very transactional; they'll ignore and snub you most of the time but acknowledge your presence when they need something. I've no idea whether the stranded motorist was one of those. Of course, even if she was, a Good Samaritan would still stop *if possible,* provided *one knew* there was a problem. On the highway of life, it's not difficult to smile at your neighbour, pass the time of day, or perhaps chat. Unknown to you, your neighbour may be broken down on the inside, feeling unloved; your little act of kindness can make a big difference. God loves through you. Be a Good Samaritan.

Weather

Windy (Ego)

Side winds affect high-sided vehicles more than low-sided vehicles. On the highway of life, big egos are easily knocked off course. Smaller egos do not need much attention and admiration; they are better at keeping on track. Are you high-sided or low-sided?

Bad (Fear)

We drive in all weathers, both on the road and the highway of life. Whether sunshine or rain, there should always be peace and calm within. We fail to see God when fear, worry and anxiety mist the windscreen. Jesus calmed the storm (*Mk* 4: 35-41). For a Christian, having faith in the storms of life is knowing—and living—the truth that nothing can separate us from the love of Christ. (*Rm* 8: 38-9) Anchored in God's presence, we remain calm.

In his teaching about living in the present moment, Eckhart Tolle in *The Power of Now: A Guide to Spiritual Enlightenment*, speaks of identifying ourselves with 'Being' itself. He teaches that we are not our thoughts; our emotions are responses to thoughts, and by becoming conscious of our thoughts, they do not control us. For a theist, 'Being' is God; for a Christian theist, it is the Triune God (Father, Son and Holy Spirit). We exist within the Triune God and the Triune God exists within us.

Worry and anxiety are negative thoughts floating in and out of the mind. Don't try to control them; instead, focus on the present moment, which, as Tolle teaches, includes *observing* these passing thoughts. In every present moment, the God of love speaks. To hear His voice, we need to *get into* the present moment. 'There is no fear in love, but perfect love casts out fear'. (1 *Jn* 4:18) That's worth remembering when the windscreen starts misting up.

Tailgating
(People)

Tailgating is following too closely behind another vehicle. Impatient drivers tailgate to pressurize others out of the way. Anxious drivers tailgate because of fear, such as when driving in fog where rear lights offer a false sense of security. People tailgate on the highway of life too. Some tailgate those not moving quickly enough. Others tailgate in life's fog instead of listening to *their* inner voice.

Do you tailgate on life's highway? If so, identify *why*—and do something about it. When being tailgated, what might love require from you?

Computers
(Mental health)

Motor vehicles are complicated; they are computers on wheels. Even if one understands their workings, DIY mechanics can scupper vehicle warranty. By and large, we seem to be at the mercy of experts. Often, the brain is compared to a computer. Life is complicated nowadays, but are *we* more complex than our ancestors? Mechanics of the mind (mental health professionals) have an essential role. However, we should help ourselves where we can. God is our operating system.

Anxiety, worry, fear and stress are increasing mental issues. Our twenty-first-century brains find it difficult to relax, calm down and be still. We are like cars with faulty engine sensors, suffering fluctuating 'idling' speeds and overrunning engines. We lack self-discipline; we do not allow ourselves enough sleep and relaxation. We have a choice, but we have to Do-It-Ourselves! The ability to reset our internal computer, wipe the slate clean and start each new day afresh is vital to mental and spiritual health. God is in this renewal. Our manufacturer's instructions are written within human nature. Are we at risk of becoming so 'clever' and sophisticated that we fail to grasp and live by these simple truths?

I once visited a garage to fix a problem with my car's computer management system. The fault remained despite the mechanic connecting my vehicle to his laptop and pressing many buttons. A costly visit to the main dealership was the greasy diagnosis. Upon returning home, a non-mechanic neighbour fixed my car for free in less than five minutes. He simply disconnected the battery, thus allowing the car's computer management system to reset itself. A bit like our brains when we sleep.

Later, I told the mechanic how my car's problem got fixed by disconnecting the battery. "Ah yes", he said, "but that doesn't always work." "Maybe," I thought, "but it certainly won't work if you don't even try." If *your* internal computer management system is playing up, get plenty of sleep and relaxation before consulting the mental health main dealership. But, of course, do consult if necessary. Find God where you can.

Mobile phones
(Present moment)

A driver needs to be in proper control of his vehicle. As such, the Highway Code tells us not to use hand-held mobile devices when driving; even hands-free ones are prone to distract. In life, we should also maintain proper control of ourselves.

In life, many lack proper control because mobile phones and distracting thoughts prevent them from being present to the present moment. Reality *is* the present moment, and reality reveals God. He is with you now in the reading of these words.

Secure your valuables
(Modesty)

If Adam and Eve had had a car, they would have driven naked until they felt the need for fig leaves. We now live in an *imperfect* world and at a time when, in many cultures (though not all), it is the case that the fewer fig leaves, the better. Drivers know to keep valuables out of sight. Yet, in life, too much is often on display for one-and-all. Minimal fig leaves will not return humanity to the once-perfect Garden of Eden. Those days are gone.

The *Catechism* notes that modesty influences how we dress (CCC 2522). Modesty applies in the streets and in the pews too. Larger fig leaves seem necessary. A priest once commented, "We like seeing you in church—just not so much of you."

Road tax
(Church)

Taxation within fuel prices seems fair since the more you use the road, the more you pay. Yet, occasional drivers wouldn't have roads to drive on if everyone was an occasional driver. Vehicle tax (which applies irrespective of how much one drives) is also necessary. There will, however, always be those who seek a free ride by not paying their way. It is also the same in life; there are givers and takers.

Many people occasionally use churches (*baptisms, weddings* and *funerals*). Everyone is, of course, very welcome, yet the fact remains that *bawefu* Christians (aka The Three Wheelies: arriving by pram, wedding car and hearse) only darken the Church doorway when they want something. Although *they are very welcome—* and this needs to be stressed—they are takers, not givers. There wouldn't be any churches if everyone were *bawefu*. How can they

81

be encouraged to give? 'It is in giving that we receive' (St Francis Prayer).

Faults
(Spiritual guidance)

Mechanical, electrical and driving faults inhibit a driver's ability to interact appropriately on the road. For example, the steering might be pulling, a fuse has blown, or the driver has road rage. Likewise, physical, mental and spiritual faults inhibit our interacting correctly on the highway of life. For example, one might have a bad back, a phobia, or a lack of interest in life.

How does one fix these problems? With motoring faults, if you can't fix them yourself, a mechanic, car electrician, or driving instructor are the obvious options. If you can't fix human faults, the obvious choices are a doctor, psychiatrist or priest. How likely, though, are we to seek professional help? Many use a mechanic, some a car electrician, while only a few qualified drivers take more driving lessons. Similarly, many see a doctor, some a psychiatrist, but not enough consult a priest.

Since bad driving is the biggest cause of road accidents, it is perhaps irrational why so few drivers take additional driving lessons. Likewise, healthy spirituality is essential for happiness on the highway of life, so it also seems irrational why so few pay attention to their spiritual lives. And for those that do, some, perhaps many, get led astray following weird and not-so-wonderful spiritual practices that take them further from finding God.

The *Catechism* explains that our true happiness is found only in God because we are made for God, we desire God, and hence God continually draws us to himself (*CCC* 27). Yet we all suffer from the tendency to want to drive *our way* rather than *God's way*. The irony is, as Ignatius of Loyola shows us, what we *truly want* is what God wants for us too.

The fundamental 'humanical' fault is not living for God. There are no perfect drivers on the highway of life. As such, consider taking some spiritual driving lessons. Be sure, though, to pick an *approved* driving instructor!

Dented doors
(Life)

Notice the dents on car doors caused when others carelessly open *their* doors. We can also damage our neighbours through a lack of care on the highway of life. If your car door has dents, you may find yourself parking away from others—an understandable reaction. Similarly, wanting to park up in the corner of one's existence is understandable when life hits unjustly. Love, however, takes the knocks and continues to be dent vulnerable. Bruised by life, we journey on.

Hours of Darkness

Road pilgrim (Discernment)

Over the horizon, the sun goes down. The hours of darkness soon begin. The spiritual life has its hours of darkness too. On the *spiritual* journey, our hours of darkness can become our hours of light. Bishop Barron compares it to noticing the brightness of the stars after turning other lights down.[6] We better perceive the inner light of the soul the more we detach from whatever distracts us from developing our relationship with God.

Bishop Barron explains that growing in holiness includes active and passive elements. Journeying towards God (God's quest for us), the 'active' is what we choose to sacrifice, and the 'passive' is what God takes from us. Only spiritual eyes can recognise these losses as gains, as light, not darkness. God draws us into closer friendship. We fall in love with God; we increasingly perceive God's will as our *raison d'être*.

What changes might *you make* to become more in tune with God? What changes are happening *to you* that invite you to respond in love? Can you glimpse the glimmer of God's light shining in your darkness?

Man, moon & sun (Satan)

Lucifer is another name for the devil, the leader of fallen angels. 'Lucifer' means 'light-bearer'. Evil draws us away from God. Lucifer deceives people into thinking he is the source of light. Lucifer is a *false* light, like that of man and the moon.

Car lights, streetlights, city lights. A nocturnal person who never looks at the night sky would believe light is a creation of humanity. When people think humanity is the arbiter of right and wrong, the false light of Lucifer shines brightly. Deception par excellence!

If our nocturnal friend looks upward, he might think the moon is perhaps *the* source of light. In the spiritual life, people also fail to recognise God when they worship creation rather than its Creator. Again, the false light of Lucifer shines away. Moonlight is beautiful. Moonlight masquerading as sunlight is ugly.

Lucifer wants us to live in *his* light. Lucifer's light leads to an eternity of darkness; he is no more *the* source of light than the moon is the source of moonlight. So be on your guard, 'do not believe every spirit, but test the spirits to see whether they are from God'. (See 1 *Jn* 4:1-6)

Are you trying to follow the light of perfect love? In what ways might you be being deceived? Test the spirits.

Night driving
(God's presence)

Don't dazzle oncoming traffic. When a vehicle overtakes you, help them, if possible, by keeping your headlights on the full beam until they are alongside. Also, keep headlights on dip until level with the vehicle you are overtaking.

In life, there will also be opportunities to receive and offer light. Timing is all-important. We are to be guided by the light of Christ within. The light of Christ from others helps too. Dazzling and being dazzled is not, however, of God. That's the ego at work. The light of Christ shines with awareness and consideration. Notice the rays of love that have helped you on the highway of life thus far. Where there is love, there is God. Where might you shine the light of Christ for others?

Perception
(Awareness)

The word 'perception', rooted in the Latin verb *percipere*, means 'to seize' and 'to understand'. Perception is about becoming aware of something (or *someone*).

Perceptions of the road scene differ. Hazard awareness is a crucial aspect of driver perception. An appreciation of highway features, such as junction layout, signs and the rules governing driver behaviour, is also a perception that some have more than others. Noticing good (and not-so-good) driving is also a perception. Despite its imperfections, the road scene has a discernible intelligence.

How do you perceive the highway of life? What is *your* perception of God? Do you ever get that gut feeling of knowing something to be true even if you can't prove it? *You* just know. This inner truth affects *your perception* of reality.

The sceptic says, 'seeing is believing'. It has merit. Yet, when pushed to the extreme, it limits vision. The point is that we need belief to see more fully. Viewing the highway of life through the eyes of faith enables one to glimpse the underlying presence of God. One experiences something of the Creator God in and through His creation. As Frank Andersen's *Trinity Song* teaches, the Triune God (Father, Son and Holy Spirit) walks with us.

How we perceive the world is the lens through which we interpret and make sense of our experiences. The universe is ambiguous, so viewing life through an atheistic lens is not unreasonable—especially in the face of so much evil and suffering. Yet, despite life's imperfections, theists discern an underlying loving intelligence by trusting in God. 'Believing helps us see things with our spiritual eyes and senses.'[7] For theists, believing is seeing.

In a scientific sense, we can neither prove nor disprove God's existence. Be that as it may, the agnostic position seems unreasonable because, as the saying goes, if you want one hundred percent proof—you will die waiting. It might be better for agnostics to try living as though they were a theist and then as though they were an atheist. See which rings most true for them—and follow that lead.

Living as a theist may or may not involve living as a Christian. Indeed, it is probably better for those with a badly warped understanding of Christianity if they don't use *their* jaundiced Christian perspective. The challenge of living as a theist fundamentally involves living as though you believe there is a God who loves you unconditionally and wants a daily relationship with you. In Ignatian terms, it is to live in the joy of knowing you are a loved sinner.

'Now faith is the assurance of things hoped for, the conviction of things not seen.' (*Heb* 11:1) Faith and reason go hand-in-hand. Pope John Paul II in *Fides et Ratio,* taught that '[f]aith and reason are like two wings on which the human spirit rises to the contemplation of truth'.

Our perceptions on the highway of life differ from each other. Over time, they change too. *Your* perception is *your* reality. Do you look but not see? Ponder that for a little while; maybe ponder it a lot.

Observations
(Awareness)

Generally speaking, experienced drivers are better than inexperienced drivers at scanning the road for hazards. This is also true for the highway of life. In addition, blind spots are to driving as a lack of self-awareness (to sin) is to living. In revealing hazards and blind spots in our life, God acts not as an over-zealous driving examiner but as a gentle driving instructor. Are you willing to be taught?

Safe distance
(Present moment)

Safe driving involves keeping a safe distance. Healthy living also involves maintaining a safe distance, this time from the past and the future. Someone once said, "Make space for the present moment." Increasingly, people realise the importance of living in the present moment. The present moment is the only moment that exists! The present moment is *now*.

Imagine three cars travelling in line; call them cars one, two and three. You are driving car two; car one is behind, and car three is in front. Car one is the 'past', car two is the present, and car three is the 'future'. When car one harasses you by driving too close, do not speed up since you cannot escape the present moment. Perceptively glance, but do not stare in the mirrors.

When you cause yourself anxiety by driving too close to car three, remember that the future is always adjacent to the now. Drive patiently in the present without fearing tomorrow. Do not let the 'past' or the 'future' superimpose themselves onto the only part of the highway of life you will ever drive—the present moment.

St Padre Pio knew a thing or two about keeping a safe distance. Echoing St Augustine, he prayed, "My past, O Lord, to Your mercy; my present, to Your love; my future to Your providence." How about you? Do you keep a safe distance on the highway of life?

Speed
(Life)

Hitting a pedestrian at 40 mph is likely to be fatal, yet at 20 mph, fatality is unlikely. We also reduce the risk of harming others if we slow down on the highway of life: simple advice, yet huge benefits.

Skidding
(Morality)

An 'ends justifying the means' approach to ethics has an inherent flaw. To explain, Dennis Pence refers to the Mrs Bergmeier case. Here an act of adultery is erroneously justified because it is the only means by which a prisoner of war (Mrs Bergmeier) can escape.[8] Pence notes that this logic can potentially so-call justify other immoral acts if needed to facilitate the escape. Pence's point is valid, yet there are times when it is difficult to identify *the act* someone is doing. On these occasions (the Mrs Bergmeier case is not one), what looks like an act flouting a moral absolute may—in truth—be a different type of act.

Consider a car skidding towards a cliff edge. The driver turns into the skid (and hence towards the cliff) to regain control. Driving towards the cliff edge was *part* of moving away from the cliff. Without considering the context, driving towards the cliff might erroneously be viewed as attempted suicide. Yet, nothing could be further from the truth. Moral absolutes identify acts (types of behaviour) that are always morally wrong. They are morally wrong regardless of context. But first, one has to be clear about the act done.[9] Sometimes, like our cliff-edge driver above, considering the context is necessary to identify the action performed.

Stopping distance
(Decisions)

A vehicle's *stopping* distance consists of thinking distance plus braking distance. In life, our *doing* distance consists of thinking distance plus action distance. Although both elements of the *stopping* distance are inextricably linked, avoiding one or both aspects of the doing distance is possible.

Some think a lot but act little, while others act a lot but think little. The combination of not-thinking-and-not-acting is an option too. The *doing* distance—done correctly—needs the right amount of thought and action. Different vehicles have different stopping distances. Likewise, people (who do) have different doing distances. Do *your* doing distance properly.

Tidal flow lane control
(Morality)

Gantry signs displaying green arrows and red crosses denote open and closed lanes. They change in response to circumstances and are often used to regulate traffic flow at different times. They are variable—yet absolute. Although that which is permitted or prohibited can change, you must follow whatever sign is displayed.

Within moral discourse, moral relativism challenges moral absolutes. The former maintains that the ends justify the means. In contrast, the latter upholds the doctrine of intrinsically evil acts (certain acts that are always wrong regardless of circumstances). Of course, most reasonable people accept that certain acts are always wrong; however, views differ on which acts are always wrong. Are there situations when an apparent impasse between moral relativism and moral absolutes has a solution?

Consider, for example, the military battlefield. A soldier steps on a land mine. Nothing remains except his head, torso, and a dying cry begging for release from pain. His comrade does the 'most loving thing'—*bang!*—his buddy is now at peace. Has the soldier disobeyed the absolute norm prohibiting euthanasia? Metaphorically, it would seem he has driven past a red cross. Yet, in this situation, did the cross change to an arrow? By that, I am *not* suggesting a good end justified an evil act—though some may argue for such a position. I wonder whether the act changed to an altogether *different type of act*, similar to how context changes the nature of traffic tidal flow at certain times but not others.

When in a moral quandary, the temptation is to justify the unjustifiable. That said, moral discernment behind a desk is one thing; moral discernment on the battlefield of life is quite another.

Lane discipline
(Ego)

Lane blockers like the favoured position, whether on the road or the highway of life. Serving the ego blocks the way for others. It can happen within the workplace, families, and indeed any organisation.

If a lane blocker holds you up, don't undertake. Be patient and, if you can, pray for them. Stick to the rules of decency, whether on the road or the highway of life. If you are the lane blocker, do the decent thing and humbly move to the left; it is time for others to shine.

Parking

Paying (Gender)

Men are inclined to walk miles to avoid paying a parking fee, whereas women tend to pay up. Is this true for you? What might this tell us about ourselves?

Space (Attitude)

Have you ever unfairly 'jumped' into a parking space? Has someone ever done this to you? In life, we should not jump into spaces (opportunities) that belong to others. While we do not want to be denied what is rightfully ours—there is no need to 'jump' for *our* space. A better approach is Ignatian indifference, letting go of anything or anyone that is an obstacle to one's relationship with God (with love). It is about inner freedom.

How can Ignatian indifference apply to your life? You might relate it to small events (like parking a car) or more significant events such as job choice, relationships, and how long you live. It is about knowing when to let go. Let your fellow motorist have 'your' space if it serves God better.

Restrictions (Morality)

Fair-minded people accept the need for parking restrictions. Applied correctly, they serve the common good. Parking restrictions can be unjust when they charge unnecessary or excessive parking fees. At such times, even the most law-abiding might look for ways to avoid paying. Is anything wrong with that? The maxim, 'An unjust law is not a law at all', is rooted in the thought of Augustine and Aquinas. I don't suggest quoting it in any challenge to a parking fine. However, any perceived unjust law does beckon the question, 'By what authority might one claim a law is unjust?'

The Catholic Christian perspective says there are four interrelated and hierarchal laws: eternal, divine, natural, and human. The eternal law is the mind of God, His plan for the universe. The divine law is the eternal law revealed in the Bible and Church teaching. The natural law reflects the eternal law within human nature, understood as the moral law we discern via human reason when working correctly. Human law is the many man-made laws that, *if just*, uphold the natural law, are in harmony with divine law and reflect the eternal law.

The next time parking restrictions confront you, reflect upon the concepts of the common good and that all laws should reflect God's plan of love for the universe.

No change (God's presence)

I parked the car, only to discover a lack of cash for the meter. Without asking, another motorist helped pay my fee. A little act of love. 'Thy kingdom come thy will be done on earth as it is in heaven.' Would I/you help pay another person's parking fee? What might our answer reveal about ourselves?

Insurance
(Sin)

Young and inexperienced drivers have costly insurance premiums because they are more accident-prone. Over time, with care and perhaps a bit of luck, the no-claims bonus kicks in. Ipso facto, nobody wants an accident, yet having a few knocks can help us become better drivers. Indeed, the surest way to have an accident is to believe you will not have one. We are all vulnerable.

The inexperience of youth is also likely to make one prone to mistakes. 'Do not remember the sins of my youth or my transgressions.' (*Ps* 25: 7) Having a few knocks in life (whether young or old) and becoming aware of one's vulnerabilities develops self-knowledge. In the spirit of Ignatius of Loyola, know thyself as a loved sinner, a flawed driver. God loves everyone unconditionally; this is our free, spiritual, comprehensive insurance policy, yet many do not claim it. Will *you* claim?

Distractions and attractions
(Discernment)

To be attracted is to be drawn towards something (*or someone*). A distraction hampers focus. When driving, attention is supposed to be on the road. In life, attention should be on God. Ignatius of Loyola noticed that when a person grows in love and service of God, the evil spirit tries to discourage, whereas the good spirit encourages. Conversely, when a person falls away from loving and serving God, the roles are reversed; the evil spirit encourages, and the good spirit discourages.

On the highway of life, when God is at the centre of our windscreen—attracting us, Satan and his demons will be in the side windows—distracting. Should Satan & Co. deceive their way onto your windscreen with *distractions packaged as attractions,* God and his angels will be in the side windows, drawing you back to holiness. Where are God and Satan in your life?

Queuing
(Patience)

We spend a lot of time queuing in traffic jams, at traffic lights and in traffic congestion. In life generally, we also spend much time waiting in queues. It would be wise, then, to embrace waiting. One way is to use these times to do nothing, to be still, no phone, no reading and no idle chatter—just be still.

Probably the most brutal waiting is waiting in the queue of love. When someone is unkind to us, we are waiting to be loved. Unrequited love particularly hurts. How should we embrace these moments? We should forgive and love despite everything, says Polish Neurobiology Professor Maria Śmiałowska:

> To love and be loved.... Love despite everything... imagine how God loves us.... When God waited for the prodigal son, he did not follow him around, rebuke him, or try to rescue him. He just waited. He waited and loved. He was not inclined to criticize or condemn. When the son returned, the father welcomed him without any reproach.... When we get hurt, we want justice.... People want justice too much, instead of mercy.[10]

To forgive those who do not love us is to share in Jesus' suffering. 'Father, forgive them; for they do not know what they are doing.' (*Lk* 23:34) God's unconditional love forgives prodigal humanity.

How much, I wonder, does God hurt by waiting in the love

queue for us to accept and respond to His love for us? The next time you are queuing, 'Be still, and know that I am God!' (*Ps* 46:10)

Hire Vehicle
(Sin)

Have you ever hired a vehicle? If so, you are probably familiar with the inspection before hand-over and at the vehicle's return. In an ideal world, a perfect vehicle on pick-up will lead to a perfect one on return. Our world is imperfect. Damage caused means there is a penalty to pay.

I once hired a van from a cheap and cheerful hire firm. Before I got the keys, there were so many scratches and dents on it at pick-up that the owner didn't bother with an inspection. It was parked near a hedge, and the owner said, "It's got a few marks. There is no need to list them, plus the side you can't see is even worse!" Despite its evident wear and tear, I am happy to say the vehicle drove well. Similarly, wear and tear need not stop us from driving well on the highway of life.

Driving a hire vehicle is different from driving your own. With the former, you can't do what you like; terms and conditions apply. Yes, you are free to go where and how you choose, but the vehicle is not yours. It will eventually need to be returned. *We are hired vehicles on the highway of life.* As the saying goes, 'Our lives are not our own.' Life is not to mishandle, but it is to use. As Christians, we believe our lives belong to God, who has hired them out to us for love. Upon our return, there is a post-death inspection, but I think God will be like that owner who hired me a vehicle. As God lovingly looks at us, I wager He will say, "You've got a few marks. There is no need to list them, plus the side you can't see is even worse!"

Whether short or long lease, our lives are bound to get marks along the way, some little, maybe a few whoppers too; yet, with

God's Human-Hire Enterprise, Jesus has paid the hire charge and penalties. The terms and conditions of the divine hire company are on your heart. Accept and respond—take the key and drive. At the end of our journey, did we show God we tried to love?

4

CAR PARTS

Glove compartment
(Mental health)

A car's glove compartment was used to store gloves. Nowadays, anything but gloves ends up in this Aladdin's cave. Times change, and this is also true for the use of our minds.

Mental health issues are common nowadays. Why is this? One factor is the tendency to fill the mind, like the glove compartment, with junk that does not help us drive the highway of life. What rubbish do you have in your glove compartment and your head? Get rid! The seventeenth-century French philosopher and mathematician Blaise Pascal in *Pensées,* said all human problems are rooted in man's inability to stay quiet in a room alone. Make time for silence, reflection and contemplation. Fill your mind with God.

Dashboard warning lights
(Awareness)

The Highway Code highlights the importance of understanding and acting upon our vehicle's warning lights; they can provide early warning of dangerous faults developing. Similarly, we need to pay attention to the dashboard within ourselves.

Christophe André in *Mindfulness: 25 ways to live in the moment through art*, instructs us to be conscious and reflective of how our body speaks. 'We need to learn to understand our sensations and pay attention to them. They are our dashboard, reflecting the balance or imbalances within us.' Furthermore, Fr. Timothy Gallagher OSV points out that Ignatian spiritual discernment requires us to be aware, understand, and take action. We must be aware of what is going on spiritually within ourselves, understand what is and is not of God, and embrace the former and reject the latter. Are you aware of your spiritual dashboard? Do you understand it? Know thyself and take suitable action.

Garages
(Church)

How much confidence do you have in garages? Are they serving your needs or looking to take advantage of you? How much faith do you have in the Church? Much will depend upon one's experience at the local level. Each parish is a spiritual garage within the Christian dealership, the priest the spiritual head mechanic!

Spiritual problems are akin to a car not working correctly. Only when one's car is seriously broken will some visit a garage. It's a similar story with spiritual matters. For vehicles, the bigger the problem, the bigger the expense. For people, the bigger the problem, the bigger the gift of God's love. We need to allow God to fix us. Visit your spiritual garage regularly, and if you need to, talk to its head mechanic. Have faith in God's franchise.

Windscreen

Misted (God's presence)

It's a cold early morning; off you go, windscreen mists over, and the demister goes on. Our brains also need to warm up to see clearly. We need calm and quiet to allow God to demist the mind. As the day unfolds, stay calm when facing the opaqueness of anger, anxiety or worry. *'Be still, and know that I am God!'* (*Ps* 46:10) Your demister God is also the heated filament running through the windscreen of your life—often unnoticed but always present. Trust and be still.

Crack not shatter (Trust)

Windscreens are laminated so that they do not shatter. Humans need to be laminated too. Our spiritual lamination is trusting in God when life hits. Let nothing disturb you.

Dirty (Sin)

Windscreens get dirty and can make for dangerous driving. Humans make mistakes (sin), and sin can make for dangerous living. Dirt shows up more when the sun shines; the same is true when God's light shines on our sins. Furthermore, a windscreen can be dirty on both sides of the glass. We sometimes think windscreen dirt is on the outside when it's not. Likewise, our human tendency is to blame others when the dirt is inside—it's ours.

Sun visor (Pilgrimage)

Most of us love the sun, but we can't cope with too much. Cometh the sun visor: it doesn't block the light but allows one to travel towards it without being blinded. On the highway of life, we journey towards our heavenly home. Until we get there, we cannot handle the full brightness of God (beatific vision). En route, by faith, we glimpse something of God. 'For now we see through a glass, darkly; but then face to face: now I know in part; but then shall I know even as also I am known.' (1 *Cor* 13:12 KJV) On your journey to heaven, may '[t]he Lord bless thee, and keep thee: The Lord make his face shine upon thee . . . .' (*Num* 6: 24-25) Do you know your need for a spiritual sun visor?

Interface (God's presence)

Scientist Donald Hoffman speaks of the illusion of reality.[11] His argument, simply put (if I can), is that our perception of reality does not function as a window. Instead, it is like a computer interface enabling our engagement with reality without grasping it. The whole network of stuff beneath our perception (the interface) *is* reality. Hoffman notes that a computer icon is not the reality it represents; it merely allows our engagement with the reality beneath the surface. And so it is, he says, with our interactions in life. Everything is an icon of reality.

Hoffman then understands our perceptions to operate like icons enabling engagement with reality rather than providing a window view. I suggest his approach resonates with Ignatius of Loyola's insight into finding God in all things. Our metaphoric windscreen, dashboard and other controls enable us to travel the highway of life. The journey becomes illusory when one fails to glimpse the deeper reality along the way (i.e. the mystery that is God).

Make & model
(Judging)

We all have likes and dislikes about types of cars—there is *no* right or wrong about this; it just is. Our favourite one has *for us* something of the ideal about it. We also have likes and dislikes about types of people, but something is wrong with this. It may be natural, but it is not divine. Through grace, we ought to say 'yes' to everyone we meet. In other words, accept others for who they are. Mary said yes to God's will at every moment. Growth in saintliness requires striving to do likewise, especially when meeting *our* least-liked neighbour. Hopefully, they will say yes when they meet you and me.

Checks
(Well-being)

Do you check your car regularly, or do you foolishly drive until something goes wrong? Likewise, living until we are spiritually amiss isn't very smart. Far better to check in with God regularly, perhaps by using the Ignatian Daily Examen and making time for periodical retreats. The goal for cars and ourselves is to re-tune and perform to the manufacturer's instructions. Are you in tune with your maker?

Breakdown
(Well-being)

Do you pay attention? Your car speaks to you. It gives clues when it is poorly. It might be something you see, hear or feel. Your body speaks too. You can reveal when something is amiss by paying attention to yourself, whether physical, psychological, emotional or spiritual.

Some car faults, such as a blown fuse, we fix ourselves. Other defects, like a blown head gasket, need professional help. Mechanics can also diagnose faults we cannot. Similarly, on the highway of life, we need a trained human mechanic once in a while. We can do much ourselves in the spiritual life by cooperating with God's grace, but we need to know our limitations.

We should nurse older cars so as not to make unrealistic demands and cause premature breakdowns. The same applies to one's ageing self. One is not the Ferrari one once was or probably never was. Furthermore, rust is to cars as cancer is to humans. The mortality of man and machine is a given. As Ash Wednesday reminds us, 'Remember you are dust and unto dust you shall return.' Acceptance of our mortality is life-giving when it spurs us on to make the most of our time.

Mortal creature, your body is speaking to you? Are you paying attention?

Bumpers
(Forgiveness)

Cars were invented circa 1890s and were not fitted with bumpers in the early years. Bumpers improve safety; nowadays, they are a must. Electric vehicles (EVs) (with bumpers) are the future of the automobile industry. You've probably driven an 'electric car' (kind of) without realising it. Dodgem cars are electric and have been around since the 1920s. The goal of dodgem cars is to dodge, not bump others. Many, however, use dodgem cars as bumper cars, bumping those in their way and those they seek out.

No sane car driver wants to bump other road users, yet many want to bump those 'in their way' or whom 'they don't like' on the highway of life. Bumpers absorb impact, and on the highway of life, *forgiveness is our bumper* absorbing the impact of those bumping us.

Every morning the rhythm of life begins, and off we go. Our arena is no fairground, yet the following theme park advice is relevant: 'Step into the arena, take control of your own dodgem car, and race around as you try to avoid the chaos!' Are you more dodgem car or a bumper car? Either way, thank God for bumpers!

Emergency services (Failure)

Roadside breakdown services are sometimes called the fourth emergency service. They'll get you to a garage if they can't repair your vehicle at the roadside. Whether broken down or working poorly, once fixed, the vehicle conforms better to the manufacturer's instructions. Same with humans too. If you're having problems on the highway of life and can't fix them yourself, friends and family are life's fourth emergency service. Failing that, you'll need to get a mechanic for humans, such as a doctor, counsellor, or priest. Whatever the fix, it will involve conforming better to the Creator's instructions.

Batteries

Flat battery (Well-being)

Have you had a flat car battery? If so, it is good to know *why* your battery went flat. Maybe a light was left on, or there was loose wiring or corrosive connectors.

Our spiritual battery goes flat too. Situations and people can drain our energies unnecessarily. Hopefully, once we are alert to this, we can recharge by taking time out, refocusing ourselves and, if need be, changing our attitude. As with a flat car battery, we may also need help from others.

Ignatius of Loyola had a spiritual flat battery when he lay seriously injured in 1521 at Pamplona, Spain, after being wounded by a cannonball while fighting the French. During this enforced time of quiet reflection, he discerned himself becoming enthusiastic at the thought of changing his life's focus from seeking worldly glory to becoming a saint. God, the divine energy, was recharging Ignatius's spiritual battery.

Is your spiritual battery flat or low on charge? What drains you? Make time to recharge your battery.

Electric vehicles (EVs) (God's presence)

As you travel the highway of life, try thinking of yourself as an electric car rather than one with an internal combustion engine. Your power is *not* now generated from within but drawn from outside, *yet experienced within*. Like an EV recharging, you recharge by plugging into God's presence every day.

One issue with electric vehicles is their reduced driving range. Two hundred-plus miles is average, about a third less than petrol/diesel vehicles. Maybe we should drive less. In life, too, most of us are too busy (often with trivia), causing an unnecessary drain on our spiritual battery. Less mileage on the highway of life will help keep us within our spiritual range.

Another issue with electric vehicles is their lengthy charge time. The key is to take advantage of top-up charges whenever opportunities arise, thus complementing a full charge when there is more time. The Church's ongoing and ancient practice of praying at set times of the day, such as morning, evening and night with the Liturgy of the Hours (aka Divine Office), is a superb example of regular spiritual charging built into the day. In addition to regular daily prayer, we can also top-up charge at any time by plugging into the divine by asking God to be present in our present. Don't try to feel the energy flow; like electricity, the divine charge is working, often beyond our notice. Trust.

The supply of divine electricity is endless, free and, like EV cars, environmentally friendly. If your spiritual battery is flat or drains too quickly, look for the reason(s) why, and plug into divine energy for a recharge.

Lights
(God's presence)

Other road users should not be dazzled or made uncomfortable by our vehicle lights. Likewise, we should be humble so that our ego does not dazzle others and cause discomfort. Jesus is the world's light; His light is the only light we are to shine onto others. Humility does not, however, mean hiding one's talents. Everything we have is a gift from God to be used for God's glory.

When the light of faith does not burn brightly, the problem is with us, not God. By analogy, a lack of power is not usually the cause of dim headlights; often, it's a connection fault, such as rusty terminals. What might be damaging the connection between you and God?

Furthermore, to work well, car electrics need a good earth connection. Similarly, God's power in our lives can dim if we are insufficiently grounded. Connect with God in the ordinary, such as work, rest or reading a book (like now). Let your little light shine.

Horn/flashing headlights
(Attitude)

Have you been tooted? Do you toot others? In pursuing road safety, the horn (including flashing headlights) is for *warning* others of your presence. Its incorrect use includes tooting in annoyance or to gain someone's attention. How well do you use the horn? On the highway of life, only toot in the pursuit of love.

Windows
(God's presence)

Cars sometimes have tinted rear and side windows; looking out, not in, is the aim. Introvert or not, we all need privacy. One's inner core is only for God; we all have this sacred space. Nevertheless, a car's front windscreen is not tinted, a reminder perhaps of the need to be open to the realities of life. Yet, we are meant to relate to others and the world through the privacy of one's divine inner life. That's authentic living. Whether you are welcomed or rejected, stay true to your inner core.

Convertibles
(Change)

Soft-top open-air driving can be a welcome change. How about driving soft top on the highway of life too? Is our rooftop mind so fixed that we fail to let the breeze of the Holy Spirit reach and change us? St John Henry Newman said, "To live is to change, and to be perfect is to have changed often." Be a convertible on the highway of life. Let the breeze of the Holy Spirit change you.

Timing chain
(Well-being)

A timing chain enables parts of the engine to synchronize together. A car's timing chain affects other engine components, so it pays to keep it in good condition. It is also wise to keep our spiritual timing chain in good condition. We need good timing to function correctly. Our spiritual and material life need to synchronize to live well. Do they?

Tyres

Contact patch (Present moment)

The contact patch is the tyre area in contact with the road at any one time; it is only a few inches. Without it, a car cannot go, stop or turn. The contact patch sets limits and creates possibilities. It also provides feedback for the driver.

On the highway of life, our contact patch is the present moment. The more we bring our true selves to this, the more contact we have with reality, with God. The contact patch also symbolises prayer. Prayer ought to empower our many starts, stops, and turns on the highway of life, the possibilities we explore, and the limitations we accept. Prayer gives us vital feedback too. Find God where the rubber meets the road.

Tracking (Spiritual guidance)

Tracking refers to a wheel's angle and direction, as set by the manufacturer. Uneven tyre wear can indicate the tracking is out; if so, you might feel the car pulling left or right. We can often sense when our *spiritual* tracking is out too.

When hitting a kerb or driving over potholes, wheel alignment can get out of line. Similarly, bumps, knocks, and careless 'driving' can affect our spiritual alignment on the highway of life. Is your spiritual tracking out? Are you in agreement with God's angle and direction for your life?

Punctures (Spiritual guidance)

Has your car had a puncture? If not, you'll get one eventually. Tyres inflate and deflate. We do too. The evil spirit deflates, and the good spirit inflates. God permits our spiritual deflation to bring forth good, such as building up the virtues of faith, hope and love. Due to the self-sealing nature of tyres, it is possible to drive many miles without noticing a puncture, though the leakage eventually becomes apparent. In life, too, we might not know we are leaking graces. We'll deflate if we don't pay attention and deal with our spiritual puncture(s). Are you aware of holes in your spiritual life?

Advanced tyre technology has relevance to the spiritual life. A Tyre Pressure Monitoring System (TPMS) has low tyre pressure sensors. Self-inflating tyres (SIT) both sense low tyre pressure and re-inflate via components built into the wheel. In addition, run-flat tyres resist the effect of deflation via their reinforced tyre walls. Similarly, the more 'advanced' one is in the spiritual life—this supernatural *gift* from God—the greater one's sensitivity to spiritual leakage. We are also more resilient in times of desolation. We have a greater ability to re-inflate by drawing upon God's grace within our inner core. One doesn't stay flat for long. How is your spiritual technology?

Perishable (Death)

Tyres and humans are perishable. Could tyres be made longer-lasting? Humanity (body and soul) was initially made eternal, but it now has a perishable body since 'The Fall'. 'For this perishable body must put on imperishability, and this mortal body must put on immortality.' (1 *Cor* 15:53) Which might perish first, you or your tyres? Know the shortness of your earthly life.

Wheel

Spare (Prayer)

What does prayer mean to you? There is a saying: Prayer is not a spare wheel, only used when there is a problem; instead, it is a steering wheel directing one's path through life. Use prayer when facing difficulties and when life is going well. Pray at all times.

Spokes (Life)

Liken your entire existence to *one* rotation of a twelve-spoked car wheel—each of the twelve spokes marks about seven or more years of your life (if lucky). Tyre and tarmac meet—the present. Moving away—the past; towards contact—the future. *Now* is life. The ever-changing present is your time to make contact with the eternally unchanging God.

Revolving (Life)

Are you an air cap on a revolving car wheel? Life turns: there are ups, and there are downs. The medieval 'Wheel of Fortune' (Latin: *Rota Fortunae*) symbolises life's changing fortunes.[12] At the top—a king (I reign); at the bottom—a pauper (no reign); to one side—a person climbing (will reign); at the other side—a person falling (have reigned). Life goes well; at other times, it does not. Things get better, at other times, worse. Christianity places Jesus Christ at the centre of the wheel of life. By living at the centre, we gain the peace of Christ; we are detached (indifferent) to changing circumstances. Don't be an air cap on the rim; live humbly on the hub.

Transmission
(Spiritual guidance)

A car's transmission transmits engine power to the road wheels. A young driver having mechanical problems asked me what I knew about cars. "Not a lot," I said, but after telling him I knew the engine was usually at the front, he said his car goes forward when he selects reverse. He was baffled as to what might be going on. "Try it again," I suggested, and so he did. "Sounds like reverse," and sure enough, back the car went! Reverse and first were side by side on his gear change—he had been selecting the wrong gear. So near, yet so far. God is the power for our spiritual wheels. When encountering spiritual problems, what on the surface might seem confusing may be an easy fix. If you become spiritually baffled, don't be afraid to ask for help. Make sure that whoever you ask at least knows where the engine is.

Shock absorbers
(Trust)

Push down on the corner of a car; if it keeps bouncing, the shock absorbers are probably broken. Similarly, taking too long to steady ourselves when under pressure suggests that our shock absorbers are not working correctly. Let God absorb your pushdowns in life; remain steady. The more we anchor into God, the quicker we recover from the pushdowns of life. Apparently, Ignatius of Loyola said he would take about fifteen minutes to recover if his whole life's work in forming the Jesuits collapsed. Ignatian indifference is about accepting and trusting God's active and passive will.

Damage
(Sin)

Imagine taking delivery of *your* brand new car, only to discover it's dented; there was a flaw in the manufacturing process. Similarly, we all have our faults, and humanity's tendency to sin results from Original Sin. Adam and Eve's disobedience represents humanity's refusal of God's way in preference for doing its own way. Society started perfect but became indelibly dented through the initial abuse of free will. Some compare flawed human nature to bread baked from a dented baking tin.

We are all damaged goods. Some car scratches polish out while others are ingrained; likewise, we can only remove *some* of our flaws this side of the grave. The final polish is post-mortem. God calls us to be perfect, 'Be perfect, therefore, as your heavenly Father is perfect' (*Mt* 5:48), yet we all fall short. St Paul says, 'I do not understand my own actions. For I do not do what I want, but I do the very thing I hate.' (*Rm* 7:15)

God sees beyond our imperfections to how we will someday be in Heaven. We are perfectly imperfect to God; that should be enough for us.

Seatbelts
(Life)

A seatbelt keeps you in your seat in the event of an accident. For most of us, wearing one is second nature. When the highway of life tries to throw us about, we can also remain in our seat. Our *spiritual* seatbelt is, 'Be still, and know that I am God!' (*Ps* 46:10) Living these words makes them second nature. On the highway of life, clunk-click every trip.

Engine
(Mental health)

Some buy cars foolishly. Focusing on the colour and perhaps the gadgets within, they pay little attention to the fact that it's a machine. For many, the inner workings of an engine are a mystery. It's a similar story with ourselves. Most people lack awareness of what's going on within their spiritual engine. Take, for example, your thoughts. Is your mind over-active like an engine unnecessarily revving? Do you struggle to switch off, like an engine overrunning? There are loving (positive) thoughts and unloving (negative) thoughts. Have you learnt to observe your thinking? Which ideas are inspired by God and which are not? Pay attention to your spiritual engine.

Oil
(Love)

The oil keeps an engine cool and enables the smooth running of its parts. In life, love is the oil that keeps one calm and enables smooth interaction between people. A dipstick is for checking the oil level. In life, our internal dipstick senses when our love level is low. God is like an oil can that keeps on giving. Don't *be* a dipstick; top up on spiritual oil.

Gears
(Change)

Gears exist for a reason, so make good use of them. Gear design matches engine speed with road speed and vehicle load. Too low a gear makes the engine race; too high a gear makes the car sluggish. In life, like changing gear, should our capabilities not cope, we need to change our speed or load, maybe both. We are responsible for making changes in response to life's demands.

With experience, manual gear changing becomes 'automatic'; you know when to change. We also develop a sense of the right time to make a change on the highway of life. It might involve a new home, a new job, a new interest, a new lifestyle, or changes to relationships. The correct change at the right time is life-giving; it gets you going!

Experience also teaches when no gear change is necessary—much the same in life. We may want a change, yet deep down, we sense the correct thing is to keep doing what we are doing. By accepting this truth, we change our attitude; the 'gear' we are already in falls into place a little further and is now less likely to jump out.

Mirrors
(Discernment)

Socrates said the unexamined life is not worth living. Ignatius of Loyola would surely agree. In Ignatian spirituality, the Daily Examen examines the day's events. Joe Paprocki of Loyola Press likens this examen to looking in a car's rearview mirror. We ask God to help us reflect on His presence in the day's events and discern where He is leading/drawing us. In gratitude, we look for

God's presence and how we respond. We also ask for forgiveness and strength and look forward to tomorrow.

Talk of mirrors and looking back reminds me of the experiential learning cycle of DO-REVIEW-LEARN-APPLY. Although reflecting and learning from the past is essential, our primary focus should be living in the present moment. Both Socrates and Ignatius were reflective practitioners of life. If they had driven a car, they would, no doubt, have used their mirrors well. However, their main focus would have been looking *reflectively* through the windscreen. Are you a reflective practitioner?

Signals (indicators)
(Life)

The Highway Code's advice on using signals is adaptable to life. On the road, effective signalling helps safe and efficient driving. Similarly, effective signalling in life helps foster harmonious communities within the family, workplace, church, other social groups, and society.

Highway Code advice	Adaption to life
Signals warn and inform of your intentions.	*It is good to discuss and consult. Some people are overly secretive, keeping their cards too close to their chest.*
Give signals in plenty of time.	*Avoid springing things on people.*
Cancel signals after use.	*Giving unintentional signals can cause problems.*
Signals ought not to confuse.	*Do not mislead others.*

Arm signals can emphasise or reinforce usual signals.	*Sometimes, we need to make more effort to get our message across.*
Giving signals does not grant priority.	*Saying what you will do does not put you in a privileged position.*
Watch for others' signals.	*Be aware of other people's signals, including body language and silence.*
We must obey the signals of police officers, traffic officers and traffic wardens.	*We ought to obey the signals of Church teaching. The Church, like the police etc., work for the common good—even though we might not like it when Church authority challenges our behaviour.*

How is your signalling? How are you reading and responding to the signals of life?

Steering
(Spiritual guidance)

Ignatius of Loyola says we need to pay attention to the movements in the soul that draw us towards good and evil. We steer ourselves on the highway of life, but what inspires us to go one way rather than another? A vehicle pulling to the side symbolizes the evil influence. Steering with ease when straightening the wheel denotes being in the divine flow. Most of the time, light steering is enough to keep ourselves on course. Use power-assisted steering by relying on God.

Temperature gauge (Well-being)

Oil and water pass through a car's engine to maintain the correct temperature. Temperature needle halfway, not too hot, not too cold—just right; the Goldilocks effect. If the car is overheating, there's a problem. Similarly, *we* need the Holy Spirit to keep 'cool in Christ'. When something is amiss in us, we lack the *God effect*. Where is the needle on your temperature gauge?

MOT (Spiritual)

An MOT checks a vehicle's roadworthiness. Testing categories within the UK MOT test (car) include interior, exterior, under the bonnet, under the vehicle, and emissions. Consider using the following *spiritual* MOT check to assess your roadworthiness on the highway of life.

Spiritual MOT

REGISTRATION MARK: *son or daughter of God*

MAKE/MODEL: *human/male or female*

VEHICLE IDENTIFICATION NUMBER: *your name*

DATE[S] OF FIRST USE: *date of birth and date of baptism*

ODOMETER READING: *your spiritual journey thus far*

INTERIOR: *How are your emotions/feelings? What might they be telling you? Deep down, are you sad or joyful?*

EXTERIOR: *What are the circumstances of your life? How are you responding to these circumstances? What are the obstacles to love? What is helping you grow in love?*

UNDER BONNET: *What are your negative thought streams? What are your positive thought streams? Do you have the mind of Christ?*

UNDER VEHICLE: *Are you centred on God? Do you rest on God in the present moment? Can you be still and have faith to let God be God?*

EMISSIONS: *On the highway of life, do you pollute or purify?*

FAIL: *You are a sinner and you refuse God's love.*

PASS: *You are a sinner and you allow God to love you.*

ADVISORIES: *You are not as good as you think you are but you are loved more than you realise. (A point based on the thought of Gerald M. Fagin S.J., Discovering Your Dream).*

Wipers
(Sin)

God wipes away our sins and helps us see the road ahead. I remember thinking my car wipers were broken. They weren't; I wasn't allowing the intermittent function time to operate. We can also become impatient with God if He doesn't do what we want when we want. God's grace is enough, so we must continue trusting Him.

Drivers sometimes get windscreen smears they can't shift. It's annoying, but once you've done what you can to remove them, you should stop focusing on them and keep your eyes fixed on the road ahead. St Paul had his weakness: what he referred to as a 'thorn' in his side to keep him from becoming arrogant and puffed up. The grace of God was made perfect in St Paul's weakness. (2 *Cor* 12: 7-10) In the spiritual life, God may sometimes deal with our spiritual smears in ways we don't understand. To us, the wiper seems broken. But have faith, 'for whenever I am weak, then I am strong'. (2 *Cor* 12: 10) Trust the divine wiper.

Milometer
(Life)

How much mileage has your car done? In the past, going around the clock (100,000+ miles) was an achievement; nowadays, some vehicles can go around twice, even more. People live longer too. The desire for immortality is within humanity. Gerard Manley Hopkins described us as God's 'immortal diamonds'. Of course, our eternal life with God already exists alongside our mortal earthly life.

On the highway of life, what matters is our spiritual milometer (*mīlĕs*: soldier (Latin); *metreó*: to measure (Greek). How much have we been a soldier for Christ? How much have we died to that which is not of God? Onward Christian soldiers.

Richard Rohr in *Falling Upward: A spirituality for the two halves of life*, talks about the second stage (phase) of life, where we learn to die to all that is unnecessary to being: 'You've got to die before you die.' He says the second stage is not tied to chronological age. It often is, yet some die early to the unnecessary while others perhaps not until their death bed.

Number plates
(Saints)

In the United Kingdom, number plates were first used in 1903. They help identify a vehicle's owner. A number plate identifies a vehicle's registered keeper, not the owner, although both are often the same.

How will we be identified at the Pearly Gates? First, no false number plates—we must be ourselves. Second, divine facial recognition will recognize our true selves regardless of disfiguration. We are all unique sons and daughters of God. Imperfect though we are, every one of us is called to be a saint. We are the registered keepers, but our lives belong to God.

5

LEARNERS

Learning to drive
(Life)

Learning to live is like learning to drive. During the early stages
of driver training, a learner concentrates on what is happening
inside the car. Having developed some mastery of the controls,
the learner focuses more on what is going on outside the vehicle.
On the highway of life, maturation involves less focus on oneself
and greater attention on others.

Learner driver

Confidence (Saints)

Newly qualified drivers need to develop confidence. Despite their
lack of experience, they need to realise they have as much right
to be on the road as everyone else—but no more. In addition, the

vehicle one drives matters not; all drivers are equal by virtue of their driving licence.

Some say that inferiority and superiority complexes are two sides of the same coin. These complexes exist both on the road and the highway of life. Humanity's inherent dignity and equanimity are ignored when money, power, abilities, status or popularity become the currency that matters. Such a jaundiced view can happen to anyone, aristocrat or pleb.

Your life is your licence to be loved and to love in return. This truth challenges the enemies of superiority and inferiority. You are loved; have confidence. We only exist because God (Love) loves us unconditionally. In response, we are called to be saints by loving God in return.

Impatience (Patience)

Patience is an essential quality for new drivers, indeed all drivers. It is the same on the highway of life. Impatience leads to rushing about too fast and annoyance at others for 'going too slow' and 'getting in the way'.

The word 'patience' derives from *patientia,* meaning to suffer or endure. The word 'pilgrim' derives from *peregrinus,* meaning to journey to a sacred place for religious reasons. *Your life is your pilgrimage.* One needs to be a patient pilgrim to find the sacred place within. In what areas of your life do you need patience? In little ways, practise patience, such as when shopping, in traffic queues and dealing with others. Be patient too with yourself in developing patience.

Experience (Ageing)

Learner drivers lack driving experience. Young people lack life experience. While age is no guarantee of wisdom, the older generation does have something to teach the young. Will they listen? The Mike and the Mechanics song, 'The Living Years', says we all blame the previous generation. This claim, while not entirely correct, contains truth. Young people can be ungrateful and overly critical of people and institutions who have helped them and are still helping them on their way. The new generation gains nothing by harshly criticizing their elders.

Are you grateful to older generations? Do you listen to what they have to say? What will future generations say of you? Your elders, like driving instructors, have more miles under their bonnet—and hopefully some wisdom too. Even the young Jesus listened to and asked questions of the teachers in the temple (*Lk* 2: 26). Think for yourself, but be wise and listen too.

Anxiety (Fear)

Learner drivers are often nervous drivers. Being anxious affects a driver's ability to respond to the ever-changing road scene. Instead of calmly focusing on the road ahead, anxious drivers dwell on driving mistakes made and worry about what might be around the corner. That is no way to drive—and it is no way to live. In contrast, the relaxed and focused driver is in the moment, interacting well with other road users. There is harmony. Such a driver is at one with himself, the road scene and the essence of driving.

Fear is the obstacle to love. 'There is no fear in love, but perfect love casts out fear; for fear has to do with punishment, and whoever fears has not reached perfection in love.' (1 *Jn* 4:18) Bring your fears to the God of love. On the highway of life, relax and focus on the road ahead. Be at one with the essence of life.

Highway Code
(Morality)

Like the Bible, many buy, but few read *The Highway Code*. Learners need an understanding of the Code to pass the driving test, but few drivers have recourse to it post-test. Some say 'the Highway Code is for learners' in much the same way some think 'the Bible and all that God stuff' is only for children'. *Dear oh dear!*

Those of a certain age will remember the recitation song 'The Deck of Cards'. The song is about a young soldier accused of playing cards in church and his subsequent defence. He explains how a deck of cards is a Bible, an almanac and a prayer book for him—for example, Ace = One God; 10 = Ten Commandments; King = Jesus Christ; Jack or Knave = the devil. Similarly, the Highway Code speaks of God when viewed through spiritual eyes. Here are a few more examples.

Highway Code	Reflection on Life
Applies to all road users.	*Universal moral norms—apply to all.*
On the road, the Highway Code is official.	*On the highway of life, God's Code is official.*
Both the legal and non-legal rules of the Code aim for road safety	*Both the absolute and flexible precepts of natural law uphold the principle of doing good and avoiding evil.*
The Highway Code is for life, not just learners.	*The Bible is for life, not just children.*

If you are accused of reading *The Highway Code* in church, you now know what to say.

Decision-making

Eyesight (Awareness)

Effective eyesight is a prerequisite for good driving decisions. Effective *spiritual* eyesight is a prerequisite for good life decisions. With driving and in life, you are a danger to others and yourself if you can't see the road ahead. Good driving also requires the effective use of mirrors. In life, it is crucial to use the internal mirror—self-awareness. Know thyself. In his fourteenth rule of discernment, Ignatius of Loyola says the devil knows of and will attack us at our weakest point, similar to how an army general finds and attacks the enemy's weak spot. Knowing one's strengths and weaknesses helps improve decision-making. What is your weakest point?

Mirror-signal-manoeuvre (MSM) (Decisions)

Learner drivers learn the mirror-signal-manoeuvre (MSM) routine. The manoeuvre (**M) consists of position, speed, and look (PSL). Hence: MSM (PSL). One should use this routine frequently when driving. MSM is key to good driving decisions. It can be adapted for the highway of life too. How might this work?

Consider this example. Blodwyn and her boyfriend, Bleddyn, are thinking of moving in together, a so-called trial marriage. They apply MSM. *Mirrors:* they consider their past experiences and those of others. Recalling the values within their upbringing, some they agree with, others they do not. *Signal:* Blodwyn and Bleddyn discuss their intentions with those they trust. Parents advise that even if they are suitable for each other, they should consider the best way to develop their relationship. In other words, carefully *manoeuvre.*

Position: Blodwyn is out of work, and Bleddyn is an apprentice.

Money is short. *Speed*: their relationship has been rushed. *Look*: they begin to see the potential hazards on the horizon if they take *that* road. Perspective develops and far better observation. Both begin to view their situation in the light of their life's vision, beliefs and deepest desires of the heart. Blodwyn and Bleddyn decide to continue their relationship but at a slower pace and enjoy learning more about each other. Whatever the future holds, their relationship has a more solid foundation. MSM (PSL).

Principal principle (Morality)

In life, as in driving, we have to choose and make decisions. Much of the time, it is obvious what one should do. Like the Highway Code, our moral principles guide us well. Nevertheless, there will be situations that challenge *the application* of our principles. The challenge might confront us in two different ways. First, you may know what to do; you just need the courage to do it. Second, your moral intuitions can be at odds with your principles (at least, the ones you have acquired so far). What is one to do?

Joseph Fletcher in *Situation Ethics: The New Morality*, teaches that 'there are times when a man has to push his principles aside and do the right thing'. The nuances of Fletcher's situational approach have not, however, found favour with the magisterium of the Catholic Church. Nevertheless, his fundamental *concern* of putting love at the heart of all decision-making is laudable and correct.

Moral disagreement between good people boils down to different perceptions of what is good, right and just, of what love requires. People differ in their understanding of what it is to love. Can you think of situations when your moral intuitions contradict your moral principles? How did/might you respond? Is love your principal principle?

Car bubble

Bubble cars (Awareness)

Bubble cars have been around for many years. No matter the type of car, driving lends itself to bubble effects. With windows closed and wrapped in one's private little world, it is easy to lack awareness of other road users. In life, there is also the danger of being caught up in one's concerns to the exclusion of others. God bursts bubbles.

Bumps (Life)

Until you've had an accident, it's easy to think you are immune. Be warned! Vehicles are potential death traps. There are bumps on the journey of life too. It may be grief, poor health, loss of job, or a faltering relationship. Life knocks the soul, our very being, reminding us of life's fragility and shortness. Thankfully, the knocks of life are life-giving *if* we respond rightly. We develop resilience, patience, perseverance, trust, gratitude, empathy, humility, and wisdom. What are the bumps in your life? How do you respond?

Car sanctuary (God's presence)

The storm rages. In the car, you silently sit. Safe in this sanctuary, you *experience* the storm. There is calmness in life's storms too. Find it and stay there.

> And when he got into the boat, his disciples followed him. A windstorm arose on the sea, so great that the boat was being swamped by the

waves; but he was asleep. And they went and woke him up, saying, "Lord, save us! We are perishing!" And he said to them, "Why are you afraid, you of little faith?" Then he got up and rebuked the winds and the sea; and there was a dead calm. (*Mt* 8: 23-26)

The eye of a hurricane is the calmest place. When in the storms of life, keep calm at your very centre. Rest in love. 'Be still, and know that I am God!' (*Ps* 46:10) What are the storms in your life? Do you succumb to fear? Find sanctuary in the car within, your soul. God is there.

Faults, penalties and prosecutions

Instructor, examiner or police officer (God)

Learner drivers are just that, learning to drive. Making mistakes is part of the process. *All* drivers make mistakes. They commit driving faults and, at times, incur penalties. Similarly, everyone makes mistakes on the highway of life—*sins,* in theological speak. Through reflection, like analysing driving faults, life's mistakes can facilitate learning and help moral and spiritual growth.

On a driving test, driving faults are classified as less serious (what used to be called 'minor'), serious, and dangerous. One serious or dangerous fault leads to test failure. In addition, *all* drivers face the possibility of penalties. Depending on the seriousness of the offence, fines, penalty points, and disqualification (and worse) can result.

Without denying the importance of confessing sins directly to God, Catholicism also requires confessing to God via a priest. The priest is there to give advice and absolution, a power Jesus gave to His Church. In contrast, Protestantism does not see the need for an intermediary. Importantly, neither denomination view God like a harsh driving examiner or punitive police officer waiting to catch people out. Nevertheless, some Christians falsely perceive God as harsh and punitive. This is most unfortunate. Thomas Merton in *New Seeds of Contemplation*, advises that one's idea of God is crucial.

A helpful image for God is that of the *divine driving instructor*. Gently and patiently instructing, He points out our faults so we can overcome them as best we can. God wants our freedom from whatever keeps us from being the person he has made us to be. 'The glory of God is man fully alive.'[13] To overcome mistakes, one has to be aware of them. The divine instructor shows us our faults on the highway of life, whether they be minor, serious or dangerous—and what to do about them. He teaches what love requires.

Speeding (Life)

Learner drivers need speed control skills. Speeding is a common driving offence; regulating speed remains challenging for *all* drivers. Many are in too much of a rush. We also need to slow down on the highway of life, especially when approaching major life junctions—the big decisions. Are there areas in your life where you need to ease off/should have eased off the gas pedal? You *may* be travelling in the right direction, but are you rushing things? Speed limits exist for a reason. In our imperfect world, even sensible drivers exceed the speed limits a *little* now and again, but only a fool *ignores* them. Life also tempts us to rush. Resist. Slow down if your speed of living is out of kilt with good sense (God sense). Only a fool ignores God's speed limits; they are there for a reason.

Wrong side of the road (Judging)

Have *you* ever mistakenly driven on the wrong side of the road, even if only briefly? Driving abroad might put one at greater risk of doing so. Have you ever mistakenly driven the wrong way down a one-way street? Have you ever unintentionally driven through a red traffic light? Most drivers will probably do something like this at least once. If you think not, have you broken the speed limit *at least once*?

Did your errant driving lead to a traffic accident? If *unlucky*, 'yes'; if *lucky*, 'no'. If your driving error did not affect others, it is understandable that you probably didn't seek prosecution for yourself. Who would? Yet, *without luck*, your errant driving would have led to an accident. Who are we to judge on the highway of life, especially when only chance separates the self-righteous from those criticised for being on the 'wrong side of the road'? He who is without sin cast the first stone (*Jn* 8:7).

Cutting corners (Rules)

Imagine cutting a corner when turning right from a major to a minor road. Depending on the circumstances, this can be dangerous, potentially dangerous or without danger. In life, the breaking of rules/laws follows a similar pattern. The challenge is knowing what rules one should break and when and why. Can you think of situations when you believed it was right to break a rule? Why was it right? Do you still think the same? Can you think of situations when you broke a rule despite believing it was wrong to do so? Why was it wrong? Do you still think the same? Your ponderings may have considered the authority behind the rule and whether breaking that particular rule is justified by recourse to a *greater* authority. These are moral considerations. In choosing correctly, theists believe one chooses God's will.

Driving instructing
(Parenting)

A child in a toy car; he or she is probably copying mum or dad. Role models are a vital part of learning and essential to parenting.

Driving instructors need to be good drivers since their driving is the base from which they instruct. However, there is no expectation for them to be perfect—who is? Similarly, all parents are imperfect. Yet the aim is to have sufficient admirable qualities to be a role model for one's children—at least for some things.

Qualified driving instructors receive training before instructing; parents learn on the job. No wonder parents make mistakes. The growing child eventually discovers that mum and dad are not perfect. That's okay! However, it is not okay for parents to think they must be perfect or try to give the impression that they are. But accepting mistakes, accompanied by forgiveness, is the culture parents should foster within families.

Instructors offer students familiarity with test-road areas in preparation for the driving test. When overdone, it leads to learners' underdevelopment in decision-making skills. They are *told* 'how to drive'—the routes—rather than learning to apply driving skills. A similar thing can happen with parenting too. Clear and authoritative guidance is key to good parenting. However, as the child grows into adulthood, 'guidance' becomes brainwashing when it thwarts the *individual's* freedom to develop decision-making skills. Too much parental routing restricts development.

Mere rule-following leaves learners, both on the road and the highway of life, incapable of thinking for themselves. These underdeveloped people are also at the mercy of other authority figures seeking to impose their will (rules) upon them. Driving instructing has a lot in common with parenting; both require a delicate balance in offering the correct level of support. Successful driving instructors put themselves out of a job. Successful parents always have work to do, but their role changes over time.

Where has the time gone? I'm letting go of the saddle one minute as my *eldest* daughter (aged 5) takes her first solo bike ride. The next minute, I'm at the train station waving off my *youngest* daughter as she leaves home to follow her career. As a parent, I hope my adult children are empowered to drive their *own* cars and become the hero in their *own* stories.[14] An adult in a real car, one hopes their role model is Jesus—the hero of this imperfect dad.

Driving licence
(Marriage)

The coveted driving licence. Do you have one? Passing the driving test is a significant step on life's journey; greater independence and freedom beckon. In addition, there are tests for towing, passenger service vehicles (PSVs), and heavy goods vehicles (HGVs), as well as compulsory basic training (CBT) for motorcycles as well as a series of tests depending on the size and weight of the bike. The requirement for varied licencing reflects the greater danger, responsibility and skill required in driving/riding different types of vehicles. Only a fool takes charge of a vehicle without proper training, risking unnecessary harm.

The once-coveted marriage certificate. Do you have one? Do you *need* one? Living together intimately is a significant step on life's journey. Is the marriage certificate just a piece of paper? Nowadays, trial marriages and cohabiting are common. People have the *right* (at least *legally*) to choose a non-marriage relationship. Christianity and other world religions, however, disapprove of such living arrangements.

In addition to theological and moral reasons, marriage makes sense pragmatically. Trial marriages are akin to driving on the road without having a driving licence. Lifelong cohabitation outside marriage is akin to refuting the need for driving licencing altogether. While neither marriage certificates nor driving licences offer immunity from accidents, proper preparation for marriage at least starts the couple on the right road. *Courtship and engagement are provisional licence time* to see if *both* are ready for marriage and to each other—*before* making a life-changing and life-long commitment.

Christianity believes there should be three in every marriage: husband, wife and God. 'A threefold cord is not quickly broken.' (*Ecc* 4:12) As the miles notch up, both cars and marriages will have problems. In the event of a breakdown, where is the tow rope? They may look similar, but *two*-corded ropes are not t*ow*-corded ropes—marriages excluding God lack divine strength. Marriages with God have a built-in tow rope, the cord of three strands. Would you drive unlicensed? Do you covet marriage?

Driving test

Would you pass? (Sin)

Experienced drivers sometimes say, "I wouldn't pass the test now. I have too many bad habits!" This is a concern since the L-driving test only tests basic competency in driving. In life, it is also easy to slip into bad behaviour habits. We need vigilance to develop good habits (virtues) and diminish bad habits (vices). Like returning to the basics of safe driving, we need to keep returning to the basics of living lovingly.

A candidate's driving test report records any driving faults committed. On the report, driving faults are categorised as dangerous (D), serious (S)—both are major faults—or less serious (aka minor faults (M)). One dangerous or serious fault results in failure. More than fifteen minor faults also fail, as can repeat minor faults for the same type of driving error.

Driving faults on the highway of life are 'sins', a lacking of love. One can act unlovingly (sin) in major ways and minor ways. Notching up D's and S's on life's highway means one's living needs special attention a.s.a.p. One should also pay attention to the M's. The repetition of the same 'M sins' highlights weak areas in one's character (habitual faults). In addition, apathy towards the general frequency of M's can make one more prone to making major living faults. Without descending into scrupulosity, the Christian goal is: 'Be perfect, therefore, as your heavenly Father is perfect.' (Matthew 5:48) Would you pass a basic competency test in living lovingly?

Pass rate (Marriage)

The driving test pass rate in the United Kingdom is roughly 50%, and divorce rates are around 45%. A significant cause of these poor statistics is that people take both too early—they are not ready. Most accept the need for a driving test, even those yet to pass. In contrast, many nowadays do not see the necessity of marriage, viewing non-married couples and single people raising children as *desirable alternative lifestyle choices*. Is that right?

Imagine a society *without* driving tests or marriage. Would life be better? Imagine a society with *compulsory* driving tests and where marriage is the *norm*. Would life be better? Licensed or unlicensed drivers; married or unmarried families. Our choice, our consequences.

Test report (Love)

Learner drivers are tested on various aspects of driving; this prompts spiritual reflection:

133

Aspect of Driving	Reflection on Life
Eyesight	*Are you self-aware?*
Highway Code	*Do you know God's Code?*
Controlled stop (Emergency stop)	*Does a lack of planning cause you to make sudden stops?*
Reversing	*Before changing plans, do you think things through carefully?*
Vehicle checks	*Do you look after your health?*
Precautions before starting the engine	*Before starting each day, do you check in with God?*
Control	*Do you use your free will wisely?*
Moving off	*Do you begin things properly?*
Mirrors & rear observation	*Do you reflect on and learn from the past?*
Signals	*What messages do you give others?*
Clearance	*Do you give others space and time?*
Signs and signals	*Can you spot the signs and signals of truth in your life?*
Speed	*Is the pace of your life correct?*
Following distance	*Do you follow others too closely? Do you have a mind of your own?*
Progress	*Are you a ditherer? Do you need to get on with life?*
Junctions	*Do you approach the junctions of life sensibly? Do you make good decisions?*
Judgement	*Are you growing in wisdom? Do you know how little you know?*
Positioning	*Where are you on the highway of life? Are you in the right place(s) to pursue God's dream for you?*

Pedestrian crossings	*Do you notice vulnerable people? How do you respond?*
Stopping normally	*Do you consider the effects on others if you quit something?*
Awareness and Planning	*Are you blinkered? Do you make sensible plans?*
Ancillary controls	*How well do you control yourself?*
Eco-Safe Driving	*Do you care for the environment?*

How well do we drive the highway of life? In what areas can we improve?

Congratulations (Awareness)

A test-pass-congratulation card once read, 'Drive safe and always check your blind spots!' On the highway of life, blind spots are the areas we tend to overlook, where we are not as loving as we might otherwise be. Personal development involves becoming aware of our blind spots—and doing something about them. What blind spots do you have?

Large vehicles sometimes display the sign, 'If you can't see my mirrors, I can't see you.' In the spiritual life, if you can't see yourself, you can't see others properly. Know yourself first if you wish to know others for who they are. Ignatius of Loyola learnt that he was a loved sinner. From this flowed his gratitude and loving response to God. You, too, are a loved sinner.

G-o-d l-o-v-e-s y-o-u. Remember the saying, 'Every saint has a past, and every sinner has a future.' Congratulations!

THE ROAD LEADS ON

Life is a journey, a lifetime of discovery. It is also a mystery—who knows where the roads of living will lead? The road ahead—wherever and whatever—is *your life* calling you to respond. Accept the invitation. Let the highway of life lead you on a journey into the mystery of love.

In this book's introduction, it was suggested that you might wish to replace the word/concept 'God' with the phrase 'Spirit of Love'. Christian theology teaches that God is a relationship. The Spirit of Love is God the Holy Spirit: the love between God the Father and God the Son (Jesus). As we travel the highway of life, God invites everyone—yes, you too—into this divine community of love. Find God within. God within perceives God without. The intention throughout this book has been to encourage you to see life as a journey with God.

Mark Thibodeaux, S.J. in *Armchair Mystic*, asks us to imagine driving down a road and seeing the sign 'GODISNOWHERE'. This sign, he says, symbolises the world. Both atheists and theists look at the same world (sign). He explains that for those without faith, 'GOD IS NOWHERE', but for those with a finely-tuned faith, 'GOD IS NOW HERE'. Faith is a gift. Do *you* want faith? If so, pray for it, keep praying and be patient. Wherever you are on life's journey, I hope the inner pilgrimage is the road you travel.

A young man once said that all men think they are one of two things: the world's best lover or the world's best driver. He also mentioned that he could not drive! In this book, the world's best lover and the world's best driver are the same. Fellow pilgrim, *your* gravestone awaits. Until then, pay attention and discern. God *is* calling *you*. Drive well—the road leads on.

ENDNOTES

1   Unless otherwise stated, all scripture quotations are from the New Revised Standard Version Bible: Catholic Edition, copyright © 1989, 1993 the Division of Christian Education of the National Council of the Churches of Christ in the United States of America. Used by permission. All rights reserved.

2   Driver and Vehicle Standards Agency (DVSA), *The Official Highway Code*, Sixteenth edition (London: TSO (The Stationary Office), 2015). The Highway Code is a collection of rules, advice and information for road users in the United Kingdom. Other countries have similar forms of regulations, some more than others.

3   Department of Transport, *Know Your Traffic Signs, Official Edition*, Fifth edition (London: TSO (The Stationary Office), 2007).

4   The ensuing discussion is something of a summary of Lewis' thought, though *his* concern was not the issue of free will but the reasonableness of accepting the possibility of miracles.

5   Vinita Hampton Wright, 'Four Principles of Pilgrimage', IgnatianSpirituality.com. www.ignatianspirituality.com (accessed 15/12/2021).

6   Bishop Robert Barron and Brandon Vogt, WOF 277 'The Dark Night of the Soul' (29th March 2021), The Word on Fire Show. www.wordonfire.org (accessed 15/12/21).

7   From a speech by John Tanner, President of Brigham Young University (BYU) Hawaii, 'Believing is Seeing' (29 June 2019), BYU Hawaii. www.byuh.edu (accessed 13/04/23).

8   Dennis Pence, 'Situation Ethics part one' (9th June 2020), Always The Truth: Just the Truth about God. www.alwaysthetruth.org (accessed 15/12/21).

9   See Paul Dixon, 'The Principle of Objectified Circumstances (POC): Clarifying the Proximate End', *The Heythrop Journal* 56(4), 2015.

10 Maria Śmiałowska, Interviewed by Julia Płaneta, her granddaughter, in Pope Francis and Friends, *Sharing the Wisdom of Time* (Chicago, Illinois: Loyola Press, 2018) p.96.

11 Donald Hoffman, 'The Case Against Reality' (8th September 2019), The Institute of Art and Ideas. https://youtu.be/4HFFr0-ybg0 (accessed 15/12/21).

12 See Bishop Robert Barron, 'Peace Beyond Understanding' (5th October 2014), Word on Fire (Sermons). www.wordonfire.org (accessed 15/12/21).

13 A saying often attributed to St Irenaeus of the second century, though its origin is of some dispute.

14 'Hero in their own story', a term used by Keith Chappell, *The Role of a Christian Father* (London: Catholic Truth Society, 2008).

FURTHER READING

André, Christophe, *Mindfulness: 25 ways to live in the moment through art* (London: Rider Books, 2014).

Barry, William A., S.J., *Praying the Truth: Deepening Your Friendship with God through Honest Prayer* (Loyola Press: Chicago, 2012).

Grogan, Brian, S.J., *God Is Right In Front Of You* (Chicago, IL: Loyola Press, 1988).

John Paul II, Pope, *Catechism of the Catholic Church*, [CCC] English translation (London: Geoffrey Chapman, 1994).

Keating, Thomas, *Intimacy with God: An Introduction to Centering Prayer,* Revised Edition (New York: Crossroads Publishing, 2009).

Manney, Jim, S.J., *What Do You Really Want* (Huntington, IN: Our Sunday Visitor, Inc., 2015).

Merton, Thomas, *New Seeds of Contemplation* (New York: New Directions Publishing, 2007). First published 1962.

Rohr, Richard, *Falling Upward: A spirituality for the two halves of life* (London: SPCK, 2012).

Thibodeaux, Mark E., S.J., *Armchair Mystic* (Cincinnati, OH: St. Anthony Messenger Press, 2001).

USEFUL ONLINE RESOURCES

Center for Action and Contemplation at www.cac.org

Contemplative Outreach at www.contemplativeoutreach.org

Discerning Hearts at www.discerninghearts.com

Ignatian Spirituality (Loyola Press) at www.ignatianspirituality.com

SUBJECT INDEX

THEMATIC INDEX

Thematic headings within chapters are in brackets

Printed in Great Britain
by Amazon

28518726R00092